Towson High School

Narrative of the Life of
Frederick Douglass
An American Slave

with Connections

NARRATIVE OF THE LIFE OF
FREDERICK DOUGLASS

AN AMERICAN SLAVE

Written by Himself

with Connections

HOLT, RINEHART AND WINSTON
Harcourt Brace & Company

Austin • New York • Orlando • Atlanta • San Francisco
Boston • Dallas • Toronto • London

For permission to reprint copyrighted material, grateful acknowledgment is
made to the following sources:

The Boston Globe: From "Trapped in a Hellhole" by Stan Grossfeld from *The
Boston Globe,* December 29, 1994. Copyright © 1994 by the Boston Globe.
Dell Publishing, a division of Random House, Inc.: Introduction to *The
Slave Narrative of Frederick Douglass,* edited and with an introduction by
Henry Louis Gates, Jr. Introduction copyright © 1997 by Louis Gates, Jr.
GRM Associates, Inc., Agents for the Estate of Ida M. Cullen: "Incident"
from *Color* by Countee Cullen. Copyright © 1925 by Harper & Brothers;
copyright renewed 1953 by Ida M. Cullen. *Harcourt, Inc.:* "Women" from
Revolutionary Petunias & Other Poems by Alice Walker. Copyright © 1970 and
renewed © 1998 by Alice Walker. *HarperCollins Publishers:* "Two Tickets for
Mr. Johnson and Slave" from *Escape from Slavery: Five Journeys to Freedom* by
Doreen Rappaport. Copyright © 1991 by Doreen Rappaport. *University of
New Mexico Press:* "Learning the Game" from *The Circuit: Stories from the
Life of a Migrant Child* by Francisco Jiménez. Copyright © 1997 by Francisco
Jiménez.

Cover photo: Peter Van Steen
Frederick Douglass photo: Library of Congress
Photo research: Tim Taylor

Contents

Introduction vii

Narrative of the Life of
Frederick Douglass 1

Connections 159

What Is Your Fourth of July to Me?
(speech)   by Frederick Douglass 161

"Two Tickets for Mr. Johnson
and Slave" (short story)
by Doreen Rappaport 163

Incident (poem) by Countee Cullen 181

Learning the Game   (short story)
by Francisco Jiménez 182

Trapped in a Hellhole
(newspaper article) by Stan Grossfeld..........190

Women (poem) by Alice Walker................193

Letter from a Freedman
to His Old Master (letter)
by Jourdon Anderson 194

Learning to Read (poem)
by Frances E. Harper 197

Frederick Douglass
(biographical sketch) 199

Introduction

"The Lives Grown Out of His Life"
this man, this Douglass, this former slave, this Negro
beaten to his knees, exiled, visioning a world
where none is lonely, none hunted, alien,
this man, superb in love and logic, this man
shall be remembered. Oh, not with statues' rhetoric,
not with legends and poems and wreaths of bronze alone,
but with the lives grown out of his life, the lives
fleshing his dream of the beautiful, needful thing.
—Robert Hayden

Over one hundred and fifty years ago, Frederick
Douglass, barely twenty-seven years old, published his
first of three autobiographies, the classic slave narrative
with the polemical title, *Narrative of the Life of Frederick
Douglass, An American Slave. Written by Himself.* Douglass,
by then a popular figure on the abolition lecture circuit,
became, almost overnight, the most celebrated black
author in history, replacing with his slender volume the
eighteenth-century slave poet, Phyllis Wheatley, as the
abolitionist icon of black genius.

By his death, over one hundred years ago, Douglass
had long been the most famous Negro in the world.
Almost from the very day he published his slave narrative, he had become known as the "Representative
Colored Man of the United States," a title Douglass wore
proudly. Frederick Douglass was the first black "public
intellectual," to speak anachronistically, a phrase he would
have found oxymoronic, since the public sphere was
coterminous for Douglass with the life of the mind.

Lionized in the nineteenth century, Douglass has been canonized in the twentieth: rarely, if ever, has one of his autobiographies been out of print, unlike the work of that other perennial multicultural favorite, Zora Neale Hurston. No less than twelve editions of the *Narrative* appear in *Books in Print,* including an audio cassette. Despite the fact that he wrote only three books—all autobiographies— Nexis lists ninety-nine titles about his work, while the Modern Language Association's *Bibliography* lists ninety-two. Douglass's speeches have been edited by John W. Blassingame and published in six volumes. And in the centenary year of his death, conferences and symposia in his honor were being held everywhere from the Library of Congress to West Chester State University, exploring every aspect of Douglass's complex lives from his role as an abolitionist and a newspaper publisher (he founded the *North Star* newspaper in Rochester in 1847, and he would remain in and out of journalism until 1874), a statesman (he was appointed minister and consul general to Haiti by Benjamin Harrison in 1889), and orator of wide renown and truly great distinction, from his first major speech on Nantucket Island in 1841 to his last major speech, "The Lessons of the Hour," on the evils of lynching, delivered at the Metropolitan AME Church in Washington just a year before he died.

But it is as an author—not as a public figure—that Douglass may best be remembered, judging from his current Nexis listings. Douglass, moreover, is one of the very few black figures to have occasioned a steady flow of biography, from Booker T. Washington and Charles Chestnutt, at the turn of the century, to Waldo Martin, David Blight, and William McFeeley, more recently. Even W. E. B. Du Bois, Douglass's true heir as public intellectual, given neither to magnanimity or sentimentality, was moved to write a poem in his honor on the night that he heard of Douglass's death:

> "Then Douglass passed—his massive form/still quivering at unrighted Wrong . . . Live, warm and wondrous memory, my Douglass, Live, all men do love Thee."

Among the works in the black tradition written by African American men, few—if any—are more widely taught than is the *Narrative of the Life of Frederick Douglass*. Douglass's slender volume remains invitingly readable, accommodating its rhetorical antitheses and chiasmus to a remarkable range of critical approaches. In two recently published essay collections, for instance, one edited by Eric Sundquist and the other by William Andrews, we can see clearly this wide readability of the *Narrative*. Essays collected here address subjects such as "The Masculine Ideal in Douglass's 'The Heroic Slave,'" counterbalanced by "Douglass and the Construction of the Feminine"; a Marxian meditation on "Douglass's Seizure of the Dialectic" counters a deconstructive reading of Douglass's "Language in Slavery." I could go on, listing the ninety-nine titles yielded by my Nexis search. Douglass's texts—particularly the *Narrative* of 1845 and, to a lesser extent, his second autobiography, *My Bondage and My Freedom* of 1855—have lent themselves readily to a multiplicity of critical approaches, ranging from feminist and Afrocentric, to New Historical and Deconstructive, to Psychoanalytic and Marxist. As recently as 1968, the historian James M. McPherson called Douglass "a key to our times."

Many texts, of course, on lives, are openly readable in this way. That is, in part, what we mean when we call a work a "classic." But Douglass's uncanny capacity to mirror the American cultural unconscious has an extraordinarily long history, commencing in 1845 with the critical responses of his contemporaries to his *Narrative*. Margaret Fuller, a transcendentalist and the author of *Women in the Nineteenth Century* (1845) reviewed Douglass's book in the *New York Tribune,* just two weeks after it was published. After noting that Douglass enjoyed the reputation of "an excellent speaker," one "so affecting through the living voice," she argues, he is "no less so from the printed page." "Considered merely as narrative," she writes, "we have never read one more simple, true, coherent, and warm with genuine feeling. It is an excellent piece of writing, and on that score to be prized as a specimen of the power of the Black Race, which prejudice persists in disputing." Ephraim Peabody, pastor of King's Chapel in Boston, said of Douglass in a review published in 1849, that "he has a natural and ready eloquence, . . . and a felicity of expression, which are possessed by few among the more cultivated, and which are surprising when we consider that it is but a few years since he was a slave." (Douglass escaped from slavery on the eastern shore of Maryland, by train and boat, disguised as a sailor, in 1838.)

The *Narrative* was an overnight best-seller. Five thousand copies sold in four months. Between 1845 and 1847, it sold 11,000 copies, in nine editions. By 1860, it had sold 30,000 copies in Europe and America, including French and German editions. And what is perhaps most curious about the book's phenomenal success is that it draws its power not primarily from lurid tales of rape and brutal beatings, but from its remarkable range of rhetorical figures, and its thematic strategy of linking freedom and literacy. Douglass's autobiography is a writer's life, the life of the imagination of the slave.

For Douglass, the will to power was the will to write. Nowhere else among the hundred odd slave narratives published by blacks between 1760 and 1865 was the proverbial "leap to freedom" so inextricably intertwined with literacy. Using a remarkable range of tropes—including chiasmus, irony, litotes, apostrophe, and antithesis—with an astonishing degree of comfort and mastery, Douglass takes his reader on a voyage through the valley of the shadow of the "social death" of slavery, a phrase coined by his contemporary black abolitionist, William Wells Brown, and revitalized recently by sociologist Orlando Patterson.

Douglass, who had purchased a copy of Caleb Bingham's *The Columbian Orator* (1797) for fifty cents at a Baltimore bookstore while still a slave, read and imitated the rhetorical strategies of the speeches of such figures as Cato and Socrates, to Napoleon and George Washington. "Every opportunity I got, I used to read this book," Douglass writes. Douglass describes with painstaking care just how he managed to learn to read and write, despite being forbidden to do so by his master, Hugh Auld, by tricking little white boys into printing new letters of the alphabet, then "copying the Italics in Webster's Spelling Book," and "writing in the spaces left in Master Thomas's copy-book, copying what he had written." The creative life of the slave commenced at the margins of discourse.

Literacy was, for Douglass, "a new and special revelation, explaining dark and mysterious things, with which my youthful understanding had struggled, but struggled in vain. I now understood what had been to me a most perplexing difficulty—to wit, the white man's power to enslave the black man. It was a grand achievement, and I prized it very highly. From that moment, I understood the pathway from slavery to freedom."

Douglass's command of vocabulary, just seven years out of slavery, astonishes even by today's standards. Words and phrases such as "vicious dissipation," "stupor," "natural elasticity," "forte," "discordant," "lacerated," "sagacity," "conspicuous," "the unconscious children," "desolate," "unutterable loathing," "profligate dissipation," "detestation," "precepts," "depravity," "horrid discord," "impudent," "cool and collected," "subversion," "uncensured," "debasing homage," "apparently incoherent," "equipage"—how many Americans of any stripe could have used words such as these so effortlessly in Douglass's day?

To this command of English and its rhetorical figures, Douglass adds a narrative technique that we might think of as the informant turned informer, the native as anthropologist, decoding the signs of an arbitrarily constructed universe. "He was not even a good imitator," Douglass writes of one master. "He possessed all the disposition to deceive, but wanted the power." In this world, the masters, so-called purveyors of culture, are in reality "human flesh-mongers," "a band of successful robbers." And the "barbaric" slaves are, in fact, sufferings of the sole signs of heroic human culture in a universe trapped in the embrace of evil. Nature did not create this world; human perversity did.

In Douglass's *Narrative,* in other words, we encounter a dramatic testimony about the social construction of the world the planters made, from the *slave* himself. It is this aspect of his text—the critique of nature or biology as the determining factor in the shaping of social institutions—that draws so many postmodern scholars to Douglass's text today. It is this aspect of Douglass's work that has proven to be prescient, part of what Eric Sundquist calls the "protean character" of his writings, and what Alain

Locke, in an introduction to a 1941 reprint of his *Life and Times,* called their "epical" status.

Douglass was preoccupied with this theme of the relation of nature to nurture. For example, a speech that Douglass delivered in 1854 affords an opportunity to consider him within the context of our recent debates about multiculturalism and cultural diversity, generally. I was thinking about this essay for another reason: I thought of it as I was preparing a short response to the racist implications of Charles Murray's and Richard J. Hernstein's spurious claims that blacks score lower on IQ tests because of unalterable, natural, genetic differences. It is natural that one would return to Douglass when thinking about the sordid history of attempts by Western pseudo-scientists to describe, ostensibly objectively, a set of observable differences, and then to ascribe to these differences—of customs, of culture, of "intelligence" as measured in an IQ test—the fixity and unalterability of nature itself. Douglass, of course, confronted this argument squarely in the first chapter of his 1845 *Narrative,* by charting "the World the Masters Made," through a series of ostensibly fixed and unalterable binary oppositions, then critiquing or exploding these very oppositions by revealing them to be both arbitrary and conventional, socially constructed and not a part of the natural order.

He returned to this theme, and to this task, nine years later in an address he delivered at Western Reserve College on July 12, 1854, entitled "The Claims of the Negro, Ethnologically Considered." Douglass begins by stating the urgency of the matter, insisting upon the inherently moral nature of scholarship.

> The relation subsisting between the white and
> black people of this country is the vital question
> of the age. In the solution of this question, the

scholars of America will have to take an important and controlling part. This is the moral battle field to which their country and their God now call them. In the eye of both, the neutral scholar is an ignoble man. Here, a man must be hot, or be accounted cold, or, perchance, something worse than cold. The lukewarm and the cowardly, will be rejected.

Douglass then sets out to establish, first, that "the Negro is a Man"; second, that human beings of all sorts and shapes constitute one species, a unified human community; third, that the ancient Egyptians—"the grandest of all nations of antiquity, the builders of the pyramids," as Douglass puts it, underscoring his words—bear "a direct relationship" to "the Negro race"; and finally, that "the people of Africa are, probably, one people."

I cannot do justice here to Douglass's carefully argued refutation of the claim, as he puts it, that "the African [is] not only an inferior race, but a distinct species, naturally and originally different from the rest of mankind," placing him "nearer to the brute than to man." "I feel *myself* somewhat on trial," Douglass confesses early on, attesting to the sense of *urgency* that scholarship—and the refutation of racist claims about the role of nature—has had for black scholars since the eighteenth century.

Indeed, I believe that Douglass's 1854 address marks one of the very early foundational gestures in the field of what we now call "African American Studies," because it identifies the pivotal areas into which so much of our scholarly efforts, wittingly or unwittingly, have tended to fall in the century and a half since.

What are these areas? The first is the demonstration that persons of African descent, of all things, are human beings, because we possess reason, and have mastered its two prime vehicles or conduits, speech and writing. The second, as I have said, is that, despite apparent differences of tradition and culture, the human community is fundamentally united. Of this Douglass writes:

> It is somewhat remarkable, that, at a time when knowledge is so generally diffused, when the geography of the world is so well understood— when time and space, in the intercourse of nations, are almost annihilated—when oceans have become bridges—the earth a magnificent hall—the hollow sky a dome—under which a common humanity can meet in friendly conclave— when nationalities are being swallowed up— and the ends of the earth brought together—I say it is remarkable—nay, it is strange that there should arise a phalanx of learned men—speaking in the name of *science*—to forbid the magnificent reunion of mankind in one brotherhood. A mortifying proof is here given, that the moral growth of a nation, or an age, does not always keep pace with the increase of knowledge, and suggests the necessity of means to increase human love with human learning.

Douglass's third point is that differences in performance, such as, let's say the results of an IQ test which are traceable to *environmental* causes, are imputed by racist reasoning, to *natural* causes.

Douglass continues:

> The temptation therefore to read the Negro out of the human family is exceedingly strong, and may

account somewhat for the repeated attempts on the part of Southern pretenders to science, to cast a doubt over the Scriptural account of the origin of mankind. If the origin and motives of most works, opposing the doctrine of the unity of the human race, could be ascertained, it may be doubted whether *one* such work could boast an honest parentage. Pride and selfishness, combined with mental power, never want for a theory to justify them—and when men oppress their fellow-men, the oppressor ever finds, in the character of the oppressed, a full justification for his oppression. Ignorance and depravity, and the inability to rise from degradation to civilization and respectability, are the most usual allegations against the oppressed. The evils most fostered by slavery and oppression are precisely those which slaveholders and oppressors would transfer from their system to the inherent character of their victims. Thus the very crimes of slavery become slavery's best defence. By making the enslaved a character fit only for slavery, they excuse themselves for refusing to make the slave a freeman.

Douglass here maintains, crucially, that it is environment, not genetics that accounts for the *specificity* of the world's great civilizations—their "different methods of culture, different moral, political, and religious institutions," their "moral, physical, and intellectual capacities"—in short, the sort of work that has become a central component of what we commonly call "multiculturalism" today. We must do so, Douglass maintains, anticipating the Balkanization arguments of scholars such as Arthur Schlesinger or William Bennett, not to stake a claim for the existence of "natural differences" but to argue for "the instinctive consciousness of the common brotherhood of man."

Accordingly, while scholarship (Douglass predicts), will eventually reveal the underlying commonality of black African cultures, it will do so in order to demonstrate African culture's contribution to the store of a *world civilization,* rather than to argue for the opposite conclusion—that African culture is a thing apart, fissured from the rest, a body of knowledge only to be approached by other Africans:

> If it shall be found, that the people of Africa have an African character, as general, as well defined, and as distinct, as have the people of Europe, or the people of Asia, the exceptional differences among them afford no ground for supposing a difference of race; but, on the contrary, it will be inferred that the people of Africa constitute one great branch of the human family, whose origin may be as properly referred to the families of Noah, as can be any other branch of the human family, from whom they differ.

The ultimate proof of both the intellectual potential of the African, *and* the central role of the black African culture has played in the shaping of Western civilization, he argues, is what he calls the "near relationship between the present enslaved and degraded Negroes, and the ancient highly civilized and wonderfully endowed Egyptians."

Not only do the humanities as they have evolved in the West turn out to have a black African foundation, Douglass argues, but America does as well. American culture he writes prophetically, coining a metaphor that would become central to our culture wars a century and a half later—American culture is itself a "Mosaic":

> Dr. James McCune Smith, himself a colored man, a gentleman and scholar, alleges—and not without excellent reason—that this, our own great nation, so distinguished for industry and enterprise, is largely indebted to its composite character. . . . (even England, that) most terrible nation which now threatens the peace of the world, to make its will the law of Europe, is a Grand piece of Mosaic work, in which almost every nation has its characteristic feature, from the wild Tartar to the refined Pole.

Douglass ends by challenging "the Scholars of the country," as he puts it, to accept the burden of their roles if not exactly as social engineers, then as those whose work is central in the shaping of public policy in this country, policy that has enormous moral implications.

> Now, whether this population shall, by *Freedom, Industry, Virtue and Intelligence,* be made a blessing to the country and the world, or whether their multiplied wrongs shall kindle the vengeance of an offended God, will depend upon the conduct of no class of men so much as upon the Scholars of the country. Born, as I was, in obscurity, a stranger to the halls of learning, environed by ignorance, degradation, and their concomitants, from birth to manhood, I do not feel at liberty to mark out, with any degree of confidence, or dogmatism, what is the precise vocation of the Scholar. Yet, this I *can* say, as a denizen of the

world, and a citizen of a country rolling in the sin and shame of Slavery, the most flagrant and scandalous that ever saw the sun, "Whatsoever things are true, whatsoever things are honest, whatsoever things are just, whatsoever things are pure, whatsoever things are lovely, whatsoever things are of good report, if there be any virtue, and if there be any praise, think on these things."

Douglass published three autobiographies; ever more exuberant about himself and his work, he expanded his account of his life in three ever-growing texts published between 1845 and 1892. These variations reveal startling inconsistencies. Douglass's memory, on the one hand, was sometimes faulty, as David Blight points out in his detailed notes to his edition of the *Narrative*. But Douglass willfully altered significant personal details, including the identities of his mother and father, as Peter Walker makes clear, even reducing by 1881 his knowledge of his father to "nothing," whereas he assures us again and again in 1845 that "my mother was my father." Douglass's texts also contain astonishing gaps and silences, the most serious of which is about his relation to his first wife, Anna, a free black woman who helped him to escape slavery, whom he met as equal members of a black "Improvement Society" in Baltimore.

Despite the remarkable number of biographies about Douglass, most have remained faithful to Douglass's renderings of his life, as if caught in the vise of the power of Douglass's rhetoric. (No one, for example, even noticed Douglass's revisions of his descriptions of his parents until Walker analyzed them in 1979.) And almost no one has even begun to understand Douglass's personal life, including his relation to his first wife, Anna, and to his second wife, Helen Pitts, twenty-one years his junior, a white graduate of Mount Holyoke and his former secretary, whom he married in 1884.

Douglass tells us almost nothing about Anna, despite the fact that she provided the funds for him to purchase his ticket during his successful escape attempt. Anna also worked as a domestic while Douglass lectured abroad for a year, supporting the family with her wages. Our understanding of Douglass's personal life—long treated gingerly, if at all, by his biographers—is about to be expanded dramatically by the work of Maria Diedrich, a German professor, who has recently made a major discovery about Douglass's relation to Ottilie Assing, a German journalist whose father was (a surgeon) "of Jewish descent." According to Diedrich, the Chairperson of the Department of English at the University of Munster, Douglass and Assing had a passionate affair for twenty-five years, from 1856 (when she traveled to Rochester to interview him, having just read *My Bondage and My Freedom*) to 1881, when she returned to Germany. (Assing translated the book into German and wrote an enthusiastic introduction.) After Douglass's wife, Anna, died in 1882, he married Helen Pitts, in January 1884. Disappointed and distraught, Assing spent months "roving aimlessly all over Europe" and then on August 21, 1884, committed suicide in Paris. William McFeeley, Douglass's most recent biographer describes her death this way: "On August 21, 1884, Ottilie Assing dressed carefully in a monogrammed blouse and skirt, put on her hat, dropped her key, a brooch with a picture inside, and a bit of money into her red leather wallet, and left her Paris hotel. Walking in the Bois de Boulogne, she stopped to pick a leaf from an oak tree and carefully put it into her purse; shortly, from the same purse, she took out a container of poison and swallowed its contents."

"In her will, dated November 9, 1875," Diedrich writes, "she established a $13,000 trust fund, the income of which was to go to Douglass," along with her library. Despite the curious nature of these events, scholars have remained dubious about the depth of their relationship: "How soon— and, indeed, whether—their friendship led to a sexual relationship," McFeeley writes, "is impossible to determine."

Ottilie Assing is the Sally Hemings in Frederick Douglass's closet. The difference between Jefferson and Douglass, however, is that a scholar now has the evidence that establishes that relationship definitively. Diedrich bases her conclusions on a cache of ninety-one letters— "written in difficult old German handwriting"—that Ottilie wrote to her sister, Ludmilla, between 1865 and 1877. "In these letters, Ottilie Assing makes no attempt to disguise her relationship with Frederick Douglass," Diedrich writes. "Portraying herself as Douglass's 'natural' wife of long standing, she writes about this relationship [to her sister] as one sexually experienced woman to another." The letters were originally part of the Varnhagen Papers in Berlin, which the Nazis used "to prove the Jewish lineage of German intellectuals," Diedrich writes. Hidden by the Nazis near the end of the war on a farm in Schlesingia, the papers were found by the Russians and donated to the Jagiellonian Library in Krakow. ("The material was rediscovered," Diedrich writes, "only when the Iron Curtain came down.") Assing's relationship to Douglass was also documented by the Prussian secret service, eager to record the movements of the radical German intelligentsia after the revolution of 1848. These materials are housed at the Staatsbibliothek zu Berlin— Preussischer Kulturbesitz.

Diedrich notes that Assing spent "all her summers with Douglass," first in his home at Rochester and later in his home in Washington. Douglass, for his part, visited her home in Hoboken frequently, "sometimes spending weeks living with her in the boarding house where she rented two rooms." Most remarkable of all, Diedrich writes, "they openly moved as lovers in an elaborate social circle, entertaining friends in her home, visiting with them, attending dances, lectures, and theatre productions together. For their acquaintances, their relationship was no secret."

I wonder if Douglass could possibly have imagined that he, even if only through his relationship with Assing, was the object of scrutiny not by Southern racists, but by the Prussian secret service! Somehow, I doubt it. (Would that they had kept tabs on Thomas Jefferson in Paris.) But Maria Diedrich's research, once published, will unveil the private life of an African American in far more detail than we are accustomed to; Douglass's private life is about to become public in a way rarely encountered in black culture. As a result, Douglass's "protean character" emerges as far more complex and multidimensional than the standard cardboard heroes that far too many biographies of black figures have sought to draw. Despite recent exceptions such as Arnold Rampersad's *Life of Langston Hughes* and David Levering Lewis's *W. E. B. Du Bois,* we still know surprisingly little about the human choices black leaders made behind the veil of race. This lifting of the veil of privacy is an important development in our attempts to recreate the African American past in all of its complexity.

Henry Louis Gates, Jr.

CHAPTER I

I WAS born in Tuckahoe, near Hillsborough, and about twelve miles from Easton, in Talbot county, Maryland. I have no accurate knowledge of my age, never having seen any authentic record containing it. By far the larger part of the slaves know as little of their ages as horses know of theirs, and it is the wish of most masters within my knowledge to keep their slaves thus ignorant. I do not remember to have ever met a slave who could tell of his birthday. They seldom come nearer to it than planting-time, harvest-time, cherry-time, spring-time, or fall-time. A want of information concerning my own was a source of unhappiness to me even during childhood. The white children could tell their ages. I could not tell why I ought to be deprived of the same privilege.

I was not allowed to make any inquiries of my master concerning it. He deemed all such inquiries on the part of a slave improper and impertinent, and evidence of a restless spirit. The nearest estimate I can give makes me now between twenty-seven and twenty-eight years of age. I come to this, from hearing my master say, some time during 1835, I was about seventeen years old.

My mother was named Harriet Bailey. She was the daughter of Isaac and Betsey Bailey, both colored, and quite dark. My mother was of a darker complexion than either my grandmother or grandfather.

My father was a white man. He was admitted to be such by all I ever heard speak of my parentage. The opinion was also whispered that my master was my father; but of the correctness of this opinion, I know nothing; the means of knowing was withheld from me. My mother and I were separated when I was but an infant—before I knew her as my mother. It is a common custom, in the part of Maryland from which I ran away, to part children from their mothers at a very early age. Frequently, before the child has reached its twelfth month, its mother is taken from it, and hired out on some farm a considerable distance off, and the child is placed under the care of an old woman, too old for field labor. For what this separation is done, I do not know, unless it be to hinder the development of the child's affection toward its mother, and to blunt and destroy the natural affection of the mother for the child. This is the inevitable result.

I never saw my mother, to know her as such, more than four or five times in my life; and each of these times was very short in duration, and at night. She was hired by a Mr. Stewart, who lived about twelve miles from my home. She made her journeys to see me in the night, travelling the whole distance on foot, after the performance of her day's work. She was a field hand, and a whipping is the penalty of not being in the field at sunrise, unless a slave has special permission from his or her master to the contrary— a permission which they seldom get, and one that gives to him that gives it the proud name of being a kind master. I do not recollect of ever seeing my mother by the light of day. She was with me in the night. She would lie down with me, and get me to sleep, but long before I waked she was gone. Very little communication ever took place between us. Death soon ended what little we could have while she lived, and with it her hardships and suffering. She died when I was about seven years old, on one of my master's farms, near Lee's Mill. I was not allowed to be present during her illness, at her death, or burial. She was gone long before I knew any thing about it. Never have enjoyed to any considerable extent, her soothing presence, her tender and watchful care, I received the tidings of her death with much the same emotions I should have probably felt at the death of a stranger.

Called thus suddenly away, she left me without the slightest intimation of who my father was. The whisper that my master was my father, may or may not be true; and, true or false, it is of but little consequence to my purpose whilst the fact remains, in all its glaring odiousness, that slaveholders have ordained, and by law established, that the children of slave women shall in all cases follow the condition of their mothers; and this is done too obviously to administer to their own lusts, and make a gratification of their wicked desires profitable as well as pleasurable; for by this cunning arrangement, the slaveholder, in cases not a few, sustains to his slaves the double relation of master and father.

I know of such cases; and it is worthy of remark that such slaves invariably suffer greater hardships, and have more to contend with, than others. They are, in the first place, a constant offence to their mistress. She is ever disposed to find fault with them; they can seldom do any thing to please her; she is never better pleased than when she sees them under the lash, especially when she suspects her husband of showing to his mulatto children favors which he withholds from his black slaves. The master is frequently compelled to sell this class of his slaves, out of deference to the feelings of his white wife; and, cruel as the deed may strike any one to be, for a man to sell his own children to human flesh-mongers, it is often the dictate of humanity for him to do so; for, unless he does this, he must not only whip them himself, but must stand by and see one white son tie up his brother, of but few shades darker complexion than himself, and ply the gory lash to his naked back; and if he lisp one word of disapproval, it is set down to his parental partiality, and only makes a bad matter worse, both for himself and the slave whom he would protect and defend.

Every year brings with it multitudes of this class of slaves. It was doubtless in consequence of a knowledge of this fact, that one great statesman of the south predicted the downfall of slavery by the inevitable laws of population. Whether this prophecy is ever fulfilled or not, it is nevertheless plain that a very different-looking class of people are springing up at the south, and are now held in slavery, from those originally brought to this country from Africa; and if their increase will do no other good, it will do away the force of the argument, that God cursed

Ham, and therefore American slavery is right. If the lineal descendants of Ham are alone to be scripturally enslaved, it is certain that slavery at the south must soon become unscriptural; for thousands are ushered into the world, annually, who, like myself, owe their existence to white fathers, and those fathers most frequently their own masters.

I have had two masters. My first master's name was Anthony. I do not remember his first name. He was generally called Captain Anthony—a title which, I presume, he acquired by sailing a craft on the Chesapeake Bay. He was not considered a rich slaveholder. He owned two or three farms, and about thirty slaves. His farms and slaves were under the care of an overseer. The overseer's name was Plummer. Mr. Plummer was a miserable drunkard, a profane swearer, and a savage monster. He always went armed with a cowskin and a heavy cudgel. I have known him to cut and slash the women's heads so horribly, that even master would be enraged at his cruelty, and would threaten to whip him if he did not mind himself. Master, however, was not a humane slaveholder. It required extraordinary barbarity on the part of an overseer to affect him. He was a cruel man, hardened by a long life of slaveholding. He would at times seem to take great pleasure in whipping a slave. I have often been awakened at the dawn of day by the most heart-rending shrieks of an own aunt of mine, whom he used to tie up to a joist, and whip upon her naked back till she was literally covered with blood. No words, no tears, no prayers, from his gory victim, seemed to move his iron heart from its bloody purpose. The louder she screamed, the harder he whipped; and where the blood ran fastest, there he whipped longest. He would whip her to make her scream, and whip her to make her hush; and not until overcome by fatigue, would he cease to swing the blood-clotted cowskin. I remember the first time I ever witnessed this horrible exhibition. I was quite a child, but I well remember it. I never shall forget it whilst I remember any thing. It was the first of a long series of such outrages, of which I was doomed to be a witness and a participant. It struck me with awful force. It was the blood-stained gate, the entrance to the hell of slavery, through which I was about to pass. It was a most terrible spectacle. I wish I could commit to paper the feelings with which I beheld it.

This occurrence took place very soon after I went to live with my old master, and under the following circumstances. Aunt Hester went out one night,—where or for what I do not know,—and happened to be absent when my master desired her presence. He had ordered her not to go out evenings, and warned her that she must never let him catch her in company with a young man, who was paying attention to her belonging to Colonel Lloyd. The young man's name was Ned Roberts, generally called Lloyd's Ned. Why master was so careful of her, may be safely left to conjecture. She was a woman of noble form, and of graceful proportions, having very few equals, and fewer superiors, in personal appearance, among the colored or white women of our neighborhood.

Aunt Hester had not only disobeyed his orders in going out, but had been found in company with Lloyd's Ned; which circumstance, I found, from what he said while whipping her, was the chief offence. Had he been a man of pure morals himself, he might have been thought interested in protecting the innocence of my aunt; but those who knew him will not suspect him of any such virtue. Before he commenced whipping Aunt Hester, he took her into the kitchen, and stripped her from neck to waist, leaving her neck, shoulders, and back, entirely naked. He then told her to cross her hands, calling her at the same time a d—d b—h. After crossing her hands, he tied them with a strong rope, and led her to a stool under a large hook in the joist, put in for the purpose. He made her get upon the stool, and tied her hands to the hook. She now stood fair for his infernal purpose. Her arms were stretched up at their full length, so that she stood upon the ends of her toes. He then said to her, "Now, you d—d b—h, I'll learn you how to disobey my orders!" and after rolling up his sleeves, he commenced to lay on the heavy cowskin, and soon the warm, red blood (amid heart-rending shrieks from her, and horrid oaths from him) came dripping to the floor. I was so terrified and horror-stricken at the sight, that I hid myself in a closet, and dared not venture out till long after the bloody transaction was over. I expected it would be my turn next. It was all new to me. I had never seen any thing like it before. I had always lived with my grandmother on the outskirts of the plantation, where she was put to raise the children of the younger women. I had therefore been, until now, out of the way of the bloody scenes that often occurred on the plantation.

CHAPTER II

MY master's family consisted of two sons, Andrew and Richard; one daughter, Lucretia, and her husband, Captain Thomas Auld. They lived in one house, upon the home plantation of Colonel Edward Lloyd. My master was Colonel Lloyd's clerk and superintendent. He was what might be called the overseer of the overseers. I spent two years of childhood on this plantation in my old master's family. It was here that I witnessed the bloody transaction recorded in the first chapter; and as I received my first impressions of slavery on this plantation, I will give some description of it, and of slavery as it there existed. The plantation is about twelve miles north of Easton, in Talbot county, and is situated on the border of Miles River. The principal products raised upon it were tobacco, corn, and wheat. These were raised in great abundance; so that, with the products of this and the other farms belonging to him, he was able to keep in almost constant employment a large sloop, in carrying them to market at Baltimore. This sloop was named Sally Lloyd, in honor of one of the colonel's daughters. My master's son-in-law, Captain Auld, was master of the vessel; she was otherwise manned by the colonel's own slaves. Their names were Peter, Isaac, Rich, and Jake. These were esteemed very highly by the other slaves, and looked upon as the privileged ones of the plantation; for it was no small affair, in the eyes of the slaves, to be allowed to see Baltimore.

Colonel Lloyd kept from three to four hundred slaves on his home plantation, and owned a large number more on the neighboring farms belonging to him. The names of the farms nearest to the home plantation were Wye Town and New Design. "Wye Town" was under the overseership of a man named Noah Willis. New Design was under the overseership of a Mr. Townsend. The overseers of these, and all the rest of the farms, numbering over twenty, received advice and direction from the managers of the home plantation. This was the great business place. It was the seat of government for the whole twenty farms. All disputes among the overseers were settled here. If a slave was convicted of any high misdemeanor, became unmanageable, or evinced a determination to run away, he was brought immediately here, severely whipped, put on board the sloop, carried to Baltimore, and sold to Austin Woolfolk, or some other slave-trader, as a warning to the slaves remaining.

Here, too, the slaves of all the other farms received their monthly allowance of food, and their yearly clothing. The men and women slaves received, as their monthly allowance of food, eight pounds of pork, or its equivalent in fish, and one bushel of corn meal. Their yearly clothing consisted of two coarse linen shirts, one pair of linen trousers, like the shirts, one jacket, one pair of trousers for winter, made of coarse negro cloth, one pair of stockings, and one pair of shoes; the whole of which could not have cost more than seven dollars. The allowance of the slave children was given to their mothers, or the old women having the care of them. The children unable to work in the field had neither shoes, stockings, jackets, nor trousers, given to them; their clothing consisted of two coarse linen shirts per year. When these failed them, they went naked until the next allowance-day. Children from seven to ten years old, of both sexes, almost naked, might be seen at all seasons of the year.

There were no beds given the slaves, unless one coarse blanket be considered such, and none but the men and women had these. This, however, is not considered a very great privation. They find less difficulty from the want of beds, than from the want of time to sleep; for when their day's work in the field is done, the most of them having their washing, mending, and cooking to do, and having few or none of the ordinary facilities for doing either of these, very many of their sleeping hours are consumed in preparing for the field the coming day; and when this is done, old and young, male and female, married and single, drop down side by side, on one common bed,—the cold, damp floor,—each covering himself or herself with their miserable blankets; and here they sleep till they are summoned to the field by the driver's horn. At the sound of this, all must rise, and be off to the field. There must be no halting; every one must be at his or her post; and woe betides them who hear not this morning summons to the field; for if they are not awakened by the sense of hearing, they are by the sense of feeling: no age nor sex finds any favor. Mr. Severe, the overseer, used to stand by the door of the quarter, armed with a large hickory stick and heavy cowskin, ready to whip any one who was so unfortunate as not to hear, or, from any other cause, was prevented from being ready to start for the field at the sound of the horn.

Mr. Severe was rightly named: he was a cruel man. I have seen him whip a woman, causing the blood to run half an hour at the time; and this, too, in the midst of her crying children, pleading for their mother's release. He seemed to take pleasure in manifesting his fiendish barbarity. Added to his cruelty, he was a profane swearer. It was enough to chill the blood and stiffen the hair of an ordinary man to hear him talk. Scarce a sentence escaped him but that was commenced or concluded by some horrid oath. The field was the place to witness his cruelty and profanity. His presence made it both the field of blood and of blasphemy. From the rising till the going down of the sun, he was cursing, raving, cutting, and slashing among the slaves of the field, in the most frightful manner. His career was short. He died very soon after I went to Colonel Lloyd's; and he died as he lived, uttering, with his dying groans, bitter curses and horrid oaths. His death was regarded by the slaves as the result of a merciful providence.

Mr. Severe's place was filled by a Mr. Hopkins. He was a very different man. He was less cruel, less profane, and made less noise, than Mr. Severe. His course was characterized by no extraordinary demonstrations of cruelty. He whipped, but seemed to take no pleasure in it. He was called by the slaves a good overseer.

The home plantation of Colonel Lloyd wore the appearance of a country village. All the mechanical operations for all the farms were performed here. The shoe-making and mending, the blacksmithing, cartwrighting, coopering, weaving, and grain-grinding, were all performed by the slaves on the home plantation. The whole place wore a business-like aspect very unlike the neighboring farms. The number of houses, too, conspired to give it advantage over the neighboring farms. It was called by the slaves the *Great House Farm.* Few privileges were esteemed higher, by the slaves of the out-farms, than that of being selected to do errands at the Great House Farm. It was associated in their minds with greatness. A representative could not be prouder of his election to a seat in the American Congress, than a slave on one of the out-farms would be of his election to do errands at the Great House Farm. They regarded it as evidence of great confidence reposed in them by their overseers; and it was on this account, as well as a constant desire to be out of the field from under the driver's lash, that they esteemed it a high privilege, one worth careful living for. He was called the smartest and most trusty fellow, who had this honor conferred upon him the most frequently. The competitors for this office sought as diligently to please their overseers, as the office-seekers in the political parties seek to please and deceive the people. The same traits of character might be seen in Colonel Lloyd's slaves, as are seen in the slaves of the political parties.

The slaves selected to go to the Great House Farm, for the monthly allowance for themselves and their fellow-slaves, were peculiarly enthusiastic. While on their way, they would make the dense old woods, for miles around, reverberate with their wild songs, revealing at once the highest joy and the deepest sadness. They would compose and sing as they went along, consulting neither time nor tune. The thought that came up, came out—if not in the word, in the sound;—and as frequently in the one as in the other. They would sometimes sing the most pathetic sentiment in the most rapturous tone, and the most rapturous sentiment in the most pathetic tone. Into all of their songs they would manage to weave something of the Great House Farm. Especially would they do this, when leaving home. They would then sing most exultingly the following words:—

"I am going away to the Great House Farm!
O, yea! O, yea! O!"

16

This they would sing, as a chorus, to words which to many would seem unmeaning jargon, but which, nevertheless, were full of meaning to themselves. I have sometimes thought that the mere hearing of those songs would do more to impress some minds with the horrible character of slavery, than the reading of whole volumes of philosophy on the subject could do.

I did not, when a slave, understand the deep meaning of those rude and apparently incoherent songs. I was myself within the circle; so that I neither saw nor heard as those without might see and hear. They told a tale of woe which was then altogether beyond my feeble comprehension; they were tones loud, long, and deep; they breathed the prayer and complaint of souls boiling over with the bitterest anguish. Every tone was a testimony against slavery, and a prayer to God for deliverance from chains. The hearing of those wild notes always depressed my spirit, and filled me with ineffable sadness. I have frequently found myself in tears while hearing them. The mere recurrence to those songs, even now, afflicts me; and while I am writing these lines, an expression of feeling has already found its way down my cheek. To those songs I trace my first glimmering conception of the dehumanizing character of slavery. I can never get rid of that conception.

Those songs still follow me, to deepen my hatred of slavery, and quicken my sympathies for my brethren in bonds. If any one wishes to be impressed with the soul-killing effects of slavery, let him go to Colonel Lloyd's plantation, and, on allowance-day, place himself in the deep pine woods, and there let him, in silence, analyze the sounds that shall pass through the chambers of his soul,—and if he is not thus impressed, it will only be because "there is no flesh in his obdurate heart."

I have often been utterly astonished, since I came to the north, to find persons who could speak of the singing, among slaves, as evidence of their contentment and happiness. It is impossible to conceive of a greater mistake. Slaves sing most when they are most unhappy. The songs of the slave represent the sorrows of his heart; and he is relieved by them, only as an aching heart is relieved by its tears. At least, such is my experience. I have often sung to drown my sorrow, but seldom to express my happiness. Crying for joy, and singing for joy, were alike uncommon to me while in the jaws of slavery. The singing of a man cast away upon a desolate island might be as appropriately considered as evidence of contentment and happiness, as the singing of a slave; the songs of the one and of the other are prompted by the same emotion.

CHAPTER III

COLONEL LLOYD kept a large and finely cultivated garden, which afforded almost constant
employment for four men, besides the chief gardener, (Mr. M'Durmond.) This garden was probably
the greatest attraction of the place. During the
summer months, people came from far and near—
from Baltimore, Easton, and Annapolis—to see it.
It abounded in fruits of almost every description,
from the hardy apple of the north to the delicate
orange of the south. This garden was not the least
source of trouble on the plantation. Its excellent
fruit was quite a temptation to the hungry swarms
of boys, as well as the older slaves, belonging to the
colonel, few of whom had the virtue or the vice to
resist it. Scarcely a day passed, during the summer,

but that some slave had to take the lash for stealing fruit. The colonel had to resort to all kinds of stratagems to keep his slaves out of the garden. The last and most successful one was that of tarring his fence all around; after which, if a slave was caught with any tar upon his person, it was deemed sufficient proof that he had either been into the garden, or had tried to get in. In either case, he was severely whipped by the chief gardener. This plan worked well; the slaves became as fearful of tar as of the lash. They seemed to realize the impossibility of touching *tar* without being defiled.

The colonel also kept a splendid riding equipage. His stable and carriage-house presented the appearance of some of our large city livery establishments. His horses were of the finest form and noblest blood. His carriage-house contained three splendid coaches, three or four gigs, besides dearborns and barouches of the most fashionable style.

This establishment was under the care of two slaves—old Barney and young Barney—father and son. To attend to this establishment was their sole work. But it was by no means an easy employment; for in nothing was Colonel Lloyd more particular than in the management of his horses. The slightest inattention to these was unpardonable, and was visited upon those, under whose care they were placed, with the severest punishment; no excuse could shield them, if the colonel only suspected any want of attention to his horses—a supposition which he frequently indulged, and one which, of course, made the office of old and young Barney a very trying one. They never knew when they were safe from punishment. They were frequently whipped when least deserving, and escaped whipping when most deserving it. Every thing depended upon the looks of the horses, and the state of Colonel Lloyd's own mind when his horses were brought to him for use. If a horse did not move fast enough, or hold his head high enough, it was owing to some fault of his keepers. It was painful to stand near the stable-door, and hear the various complaints against the keepers when a horse was taken out for use. "This horse has not had proper attention. He has not been sufficiently rubbed and curried, or he has not been properly fed; his food was too wet or too dry; he got it too soon or too late; he was too hot or too cold; he had too much hay, and not enough of grain; or he had too much grain, and not enough of hay; instead of old Barney's attending to the horse, he had very improperly left it to his son." To all these complaints, no matter how unjust, the slave must answer never a word. Colonel Lloyd could not brook any contradiction from a slave. When he spoke, a slave must stand, listen, and tremble; and such was literally the case. I have seen Colonel Lloyd make old Barney, a man between fifty and sixty years of age, uncover his bald head, kneel down upon the cold, damp ground, and receive upon his naked and toil-worn shoulders more than thirty lashes at the time. Colonel Lloyd had three sons—Edward, Murray, and Daniel,—and three sons-in-law, Mr. Winder, Mr. Nicholson, and Mr. Lowndes. All of these lived at the Great House Farm, and enjoyed the luxury of whipping the servants when they pleased, from old Barney down to William Wilkes, the coach-driver. I have seen Winder make one of the house-servants stand off from him a suitable distance to be touched with the end of his whip, and at every stroke raise great ridges upon his back.

To describe the wealth of Colonel Lloyd would be almost equal to describing the riches of Job. He kept from ten to fifteen house-servants. He was said to own a thousand slaves, and I think this estimate quite within the truth. Colonel Lloyd owned so many that he did not know them when he saw them; nor did all the slaves of the out-farms know him. It is reported to him, that, while riding along the road one day, he met a colored man, and addressed him in the usual manner of speaking to colored people on the public highways of the south: "Well, boy, whom do you belong to?" "To Colonel Lloyd," replied the slave. "Well, does the colonel treat you well?" "No, sir," was the ready reply. "What, does he work you too hard?" "Yes, sir." "Well, don't he give you enough to eat?" "Yes, sir, he gives me enough, such as it is."

The colonel, after ascertaining where the slave belonged, rode on; the man also went on about his business, not dreaming that he had been conversing with his master. He thought, said, and heard nothing more of the matter, until two or three weeks afterwards. The poor man was then informed by his overseer that, for having found fault with his master, he was now to be sold to a Georgia trader. He was immediately chained and handcuffed; and thus, without a moment's warning, he was snatched away, and forever sundered, from his family and friends, by a hand more unrelenting than death. This is the penalty of telling the truth, of telling the simple truth, in answer to a series of plain questions.

It is partly in consequence of such facts, that slaves, when inquired of as to their condition and the character of their masters, almost universally say they are contented, and that their masters are kind. The slaveholders have been known to send in spies among their slaves, to ascertain their views and feelings in regard to their condition. The frequency of this has had the effect to establish among the slaves the maxim, that a still tongue makes a wise head. They suppress the truth rather than take the consequences of telling it, and in so doing prove themselves a part of the human family. If they have any thing to say of their masters, it is generally in their masters' favor, especially when speaking to an untried man. I have been frequently asked, when a slave, if I had a kind master, and do not remember ever to have given a negative answer; nor did I, in pursuing this course, consider myself as uttering what was absolutely false; for I always measured the kindness of my master by the standard of kindness set up among slaveholders around us. Moreover, slaves are like other people, and imbibe prejudices quite common to others. They think their own better than that of others. Many, under the influence of this prejudice, think their own masters are better than the masters of other slaves; and this, too, in some cases, when the very reverse is true. Indeed, it is not uncommon for slaves even to fall out and quarrel among themselves about the relative goodness of their masters, each contending for the superior goodness of his own over that of the others. At the very same time, they mutually execrate their masters when viewed separately. It was so on our plantation. When Colonel Lloyd's slaves met the slaves of Jacob Jepson, they seldom parted without a quarrel about their masters; Colonel Lloyd's slaves contending that he was the richest, and Mr. Jepson's slaves that he was the smartest, and most of a man. Colonel Lloyd's slaves would boast his ability to buy and sell Jacob Jepson. Mr. Jepson's slaves would boast his ability to whip Colonel Lloyd. These quarrels would almost always end in a fight between the parties, and those that whipped were supposed to have gained the point at issue. They seemed to think that the greatness of their masters was transferable to themselves. It was considered as being bad enough to be a slave; but to be a poor man's slave was deemed a disgrace indeed!

CHAPTER IV

MR. HOPKINS remained but a short time in the office of overseer. Why his career was so short, I do not know, but suppose he lacked the necessary severity to suit Colonel Lloyd. Mr. Hopkins was succeeded by Mr. Austin Gore, a man possessing, in an eminent degree, all those traits of character indispensable to what is called a first-rate overseer. Mr. Gore had served Colonel Lloyd, in the capacity of overseer, upon one of the out-farms, and had shown himself worthy of the high station of overseer upon the home or Great House Farm.

Mr. Gore was proud, ambitious, and persevering. He was artful, cruel, and obdurate. He was just the man for such a place, and it was just the place for such a man. It afforded scope for the full exercise of all his powers, and he seemed to be perfectly at home in it. He was one of those who could torture the slightest look, word, or gesture, on the part of the slave, into impudence, and would treat it accordingly. There must be no answering back to him; no explanation was allowed a slave, showing himself to have been wrongfully accused. Mr. Gore acted fully up to the maxim laid down by slaveholders,—"It is better that a dozen slaves suffer under the lash, than that the overseer should be convicted, in the presence of the slaves, or having been at fault." No matter how innocent a slave might be—it availed him nothing, when accused by Mr. Gore of any misdemeanor. To be accused was to be convicted, and to be convicted was to be punished; the one always following the other with immutable certainty. To escape punishment was to escape accusation; and few slaves had the fortune to do either, under the overseership of Mr. Gore. He was just proud enough to demand the most debasing homage of the slave, and quite servile enough to crouch, himself, at the feet of the master. He was ambitious enough to be contented with nothing short of the highest rank of overseers, and persevering enough to reach the height of his ambition. He was cruel enough to inflict the severest punishment, artful enough to descend to the lowest trickery, and obdurate enough to be insensible to the voice of a reproving conscience. He was, of all the overseers, the most dreaded by the slaves. His presence was painful; his eye flashed confusion; and seldom was his sharp, shrill voice heard, without producing horror and trembling in their ranks.

Mr. Gore was a grave man, and, though a young man, he indulged in no jokes, said no funny words, seldom smiled. His words were in perfect keeping with his looks, and his looks were in perfect keeping with his words. Overseers will sometimes indulge in a witty word, even with the slaves; not so with Mr. Gore. He spoke but to command, and commanded but to be obeyed; he dealt sparingly with his words, and bountifully with his whip, never using the former where the latter would answer as well. When he whipped, he seemed to do so from a sense of duty, and feared no consequences. He did nothing reluctantly, no matter how disagreeable; always at his post, never inconsistent. He never promised but to fulfil. He was, in a word, a man of the most inflexible firmness and stone-like coolness.

His savage barbarity was equalled only by the consummate coolness with which he committed the grossest and most savage deeds upon the slaves under his charge. Mr. Gore once undertook to whip one of Colonel Lloyd's slaves, by the name of Demby. He had given Demby but few stripes, when, to get rid of the scourging, he ran and plunged himself into a creek, and stood there at the depth of his shoulders, refusing to come out. Mr. Gore told him that he would give him three calls, and that, if he did not come out at the third call, he would shoot him. The first call was given. Demby made no response, but stood his ground. The second and third calls were given with the same result. Mr. Gore then, without consultation or deliberation with any one, not even giving Demby an additional call, raised his musket to his face, taking deadly aim at his standing victim, and in an instant poor Demby was no more. His mangled body sank out of sight, and blood and brains marked the water where he had stood.

A thrill of horror flashed through every soul upon the plantation, excepting Mr. Gore. He alone seemed cool and collected. He was asked by Colonel Lloyd and my old master, why he resorted to this extraordinary expedient. His reply was, (as well as I can remember,) that Demby had become unmanageable. He was setting a dangerous example to the other slaves,—one which, if suffered to pass without some such demonstration on his part, would finally lead to the total subversion of all rule and order upon the plantation. He argued that if one slave refused to be corrected, and escaped with his life, the other slaves would soon copy the example; the result of which would be, the freedom of the slaves, and the enslavement of the whites. Mr. Gore's defence was satisfactory. He was continued in his station as overseer upon the home plantation. His fame as an overseer went abroad. His horrid crime was not even submitted to judicial investigation. It was committed in the presence of slaves, and they of course could neither institute a suit, nor testify against him; and thus the guilty perpetrator of one of the bloodiest and most foul murders goes unwhipped of justice, and uncensured by the community in which he lives. Mr. Gore lived in St. Michael's, Talbot county, Maryland, when I left there; and if he is still alive, he very probably lives there now; and if so, he is now, as he was then, as highly esteemed and as much respected as though his guilty soul had not been stained with his brother's blood.

I speak advisedly when I say this,—that killing a slave, or any colored person, in Talbot county, Maryland, is not treated as a crime, either by the courts or the community. Mr. Thomas Lanman, of St. Michael's, killed two slaves, one of whom he killed with a hatchet, by knocking his brains out. He used to boast of the commission of the awful and bloody deed. I have heard him do so laughingly, saying, among other things, that he was the only benefactor of his country in the company, and that when others would do as much as he had done, we should be relieved of "the d—d niggers."

The wife of Mr. Giles Hicks, living but a short distance from where I used to live, murdered my wife's cousin, a young girl between fifteen and sixteen years of age, mangling her person in the most horrible manner, breaking her nose and breastbone with a stick, so that the poor girl expired in a few hours afterward. She was immediately buried, but had not been in her untimely grave but a few hours before she was taken up and examined by the coroner, who decided that she had come to her death by severe beating. The offence for which this girl was thus murdered was this:—She had been set that night to mind Mrs. Hicks's baby, and during the night she fell asleep, and the baby cried. She, having lost her rest for several nights previous, did not hear the crying. They were both in the room with Mrs. Hicks. Mrs. Hicks, finding the girl slow to move, jumped from her bed, seized an oak stick of wood by the fireplace, and with it broke the girl's nose and breastbone, and thus ended her life. I will not say that this most horrid murder produced no sensation in the community. It did produce sensation, but not enough to bring the murderess to punishment. There was a warrant issued for her arrest, but it was never served. Thus she escaped not only punishment, but even the pain of being arraigned before a court for her horrid crime.

Whilst I am detailing bIoody deeds which took place during my stay on Colonel Lloyd's plantation, I will briefly narrate another, which occurred about the same time as the murder of Demby by Mr. Gore.

Colonel Lloyd's slaves were in the habit of spending a part of their nights and Sundays in fishing for oysters, and in this way made up the deficiency of their scanty allowance. An old man belonging to Colonel Lloyd, while thus engaged, happened to get beyond the limits of Colonel Lloyd's, and on the premises of Mr. Beal Bondly. At this trespass, Mr. Bondly took offence, and with his musket came down to the shore, and blew its deadly contents into the poor old man.

Mr. Bondly came over to see Colonel Lloyd the next day, whether to pay him for his property, or to justify himself in what he had done, I know not. At any rate, this whole fiendish transaction was soon hushed up. There was very little said about it at all, and nothing done. It was a common saying, even among little white boys, that it was worth a half-cent to kill a "nigger," and a half-cent to bury one.

CHAPTER V

As to my own treatment while I lived on Colonel Lloyd's plantation, it was very similar to that of the other slave children. I was not old enough to work in the field, and there being little else than field work to do, I had a great deal of leisure time. The most I had to do was to drive up the cows at evening, keep the fowls out of the garden, keep the front yard clean, and run of errands for my old master's daughter, Mrs. Lucretia Auld. The most of my leisure time I spent in helping Master Daniel Lloyd in finding his birds, after he had shot them. My connection with Master Daniel was of some advantage to me. He became quite attached to me, and was a sort of protector of me. He would not allow the older boys to impose upon me, and would divide his cakes with me.

I was seldom whipped by my old master, and suffered little from any thing else than hunger and cold. I suffered much from hunger, but much more from cold. In hottest summer and coldest winter, I was kept almost naked—no shoes, no stockings, no jacket, no trousers, nothing on but a coarse tow linen shirt, reaching only to my knees. I had no bed. I must have perished with cold, but that, the coldest nights, I used to steal a bag which was used for carrying corn to the mill. I would crawl into this bag, and there sleep on the cold, damp, clay floor, with my head in and feet out. My feet have been so cracked with the frost, that the pen with which I am writing might be laid in the gashes.

We were not regularly allowanced. Our food was coarse corn meal boiled. This was called *mush*. It was put into a large wooden tray or trough, and set down upon the ground. The children were then called, like so many pigs, and like so many pigs they would come and devour the mush; some with oyster-shells, others with pieces of shingle, some with naked hands, and none with spoons. He that ate fastest got most; he that was strongest secured the best place; and few left the trough satisfied.

I was probably between seven and eight years old when I left Colonel Lloyd's plantation. I left it with joy. I shall never forget the ecstasy with which I received the intelligence that my old master (Anthony) had determined to let me go to Baltimore, to live with Mr. Hugh Auld, brother to my old master's son-in-law, Captain Thomas Auld. I received this information about three days before my departure. They were three of the happiest days I ever enjoyed. I spent the most part of all these three days in the creek, washing off the plantation scurf, and preparing myself for my departure.

The pride of appearance which this would indicate was not my own. I spent the time in washing, not so much because I wished to, but because Mrs. Lucretia had told me I must get all the dead skin off my feet and knees before I could go to Baltimore; for the people in Baltimore were very cleanly, and would laugh at me if I looked dirty. Besides, she was going to give me a pair of trousers, which I should not put on unless I got all the dirt off me. The thought of owning a pair of trousers was great indeed! It was almost a sufficient motive, not only to make me take off what would be called by pig-drovers the mange, but the skin itself. I went at it in good earnest, working for the first time with the hope of reward.

The ties that ordinarily bind children to their homes were all suspended in my case. I found no severe trial in my departure. My home was charmless; it was not home to me; on parting from it, I could not feel that I was leaving any thing which I could have enjoyed by staying. My mother was dead, my grandmother lived far off, so that I seldom saw her. I had two sisters and one brother, that lived in the same house with me; but the early separation of us from our mother had well nigh blotted the fact of our relationship from our memories. I looked for home elsewhere, and was confident of finding none which I should relish less than the one which I was leaving. If, however, I found in my new home hardship, hunger, whipping, and nakedness, I had the consolation that I should not have escaped any one of them by staying. Having already had more than a taste of them in the house of my old master, and having endured them there, I very naturally inferred my ability to endure them elsewhere, and especially at Baltimore; for I had something of the feeling about Baltimore that is expressed in the proverb, that "being hanged in England is preferable to dying a natural death in Ireland." I had the strongest desire to see Baltimore. Cousin Tom, though not fluent in speech, had inspired me with that desire by his eloquent description of the place. I could never point out any thing at the Great House, no matter how beautiful or powerful, but that he had seen something at Baltimore far exceeding, both in beauty and strength, the object which I pointed out to him.

Even the Great House itself, with all its pictures, was far inferior to many buildings in Baltimore. So strong was my desire, that I thought a gratification of it would fully compensate for whatever loss of comforts I should sustain by the exchange. I left without a regret, and with the highest hopes of future happiness.

We sailed out of Miles River for Baltimore on a Saturday morning. I remember only the day of the week, for at that time I had no knowledge of the days of the month, nor the months of the year. On setting sail, I walked aft, and gave to Colonel Lloyd's plantation what I hoped would be the last look. I then placed myself in the bows of the sloop, and there spent the remainder of the day in looking ahead, interesting myself in what was in the distance rather than in things near by or behind.

In the afternoon of that day, we reached Annapolis, the capital of the State. We stopped but a few moments, so that I had no time to go on shore. It was the first large town that I had ever seen, and though it would look small compared with some of our New England factory villages, I thought it a wonderful place for its size—more imposing even than the Great House Farm!

We arrived at Baltimore early on Sunday morning, landing at Smith's Wharf, not far from Bowley's Wharf. We had on board the sloop a large flock of sheep; and after aiding in driving them to the slaughterhouse of Mr. Curtis on Louden Slater's Hill, I was conducted by Rich, one of the hands belonging on board of the sloop, to my new home in Alliciana Street, near Mr. Gardner's shipyard, on Fells Point.

Mr. and Mrs. Auld were both at home, and met me at the door with their little son Thomas, to take care of whom I had been given. And here I saw what I had never seen before; it was a white face beaming with the most kindly emotions; it was the face of my new mistress, Sophia Auld. I wish I could describe the rapture that flashed through my soul as I beheld it. It was a new and strange sight to me, brightening up my pathway with the light of happiness. Little Thomas was told, there was his Freddy,—and I was told to take care of little Thomas; and thus I entered upon the duties of my new home with the most cheering prospect ahead.

I look upon my departure from Colonel Lloyd's plantation as one of the most interesting events of my life. It is possible, and even quite probable, that but for the mere circumstance of being removed from that plantation to Baltimore, I should have to-day, instead of being here seated by my own table, in the enjoyment of freedom and the happiness of home, writing this Narrative, been confined in the galling chains of slavery. Going to live at Baltimore laid the foundation, and opened the gateway, to all my subsequent prosperity. I have ever regarded it as the first plain manifestation of that kind providence which has ever since attended me, and marked my life with so many favors. I regarded the selection of myself as being somewhat remarkable. There were a number of slave children that might have been sent from the plantation to Baltimore. There were those younger, those older, and those of the same age. I was chosen from among them all, and was the first, last, and only choice.

I may be deemed superstitious, and even egotistical, in regarding this event as a special interposition of divine Providence in my favor. But I should be false to the earliest sentiments of my soul, if I suppressed the opinion. I prefer to be true to myself, even at the hazard of incurring the ridicule of others, rather than to be false, and incur my own abhorrence From my earliest recollection, I date the entertainment of a deep conviction that slavery would not always be able to hold me within its foul embrace; and in the darkest hours of my career in slavery, this living word of faith and spirit of hope departed not from me, but remained like ministering angels to cheer me through the gloom. This good spirit was from God, and to him I offer thanksgiving and praise.

CHAPTER VI

MY new mistress proved to be all she appeared when I first met her at the door,—a woman of the kindest heart and finest feelings. She had never had a slave under her control previously to myself, and prior to her marriage she had been dependent upon her own industry for a living. She was by trade a weaver; and by constant application to her business, she had been in a good degree preserved from the blighting and dehumanizing effects of slavery. I was utterly astonished at her goodness. I scarcely knew how to behave towards her. She was entirely unlike any other white woman I had ever seen. I could not approach her as I was accustomed to approach other white ladies. My early instruction was all out of place. The crouching servility, usually so acceptable a quality in a slave, did not answer when manifested toward her. Her favor was not gained by it; she seemed to be disturbed by it. She did not deem it impudent or unmannerly for a slave to look her in the face. The meanest slave was put fully at ease in her presence, and none left without feeling better for having seen her. Her face was made of heavenly smiles, and her voice of tranquil music.

But, alas! this kind heart had but a short time to remain such. The fatal poison of irresponsible power was already in her hands, and soon commenced its infernal work. That cheerful eye, under the influence of slavery, soon became red with rage; that voice, made all of sweet accord, changed to one of harsh and horrid discord; and that angelic face gave place to that of a demon.

Very soon after I went to live with Mr. and Mrs. Auld, she very kindly commenced to teach me the A, B, C. After I had learned this, she assisted me in learning to spell words of three or four letters. Just at this point of my progress, Mr. Auld found out what was going on, and at once forbade Mrs. Auld to instruct me further, telling her, among other things, that it was unlawful, as well as unsafe, to teach a slave to read. To use his own words, further, he said, "If you give a nigger an inch, he will take an ell. A nigger should know nothing but to obey his master—to do as he is told to do. Learning would *spoil* the best nigger in the world. Now," said he, "if you teach that nigger (speaking of myself) how to read, there would be no keeping him. It would forever unfit him to be a slave. He would at once become unmanageable, and of no value to his master. As to himself, it could do him no good, but a great deal of harm. It would make him discontented and unhappy." These words sank deep into my heart, stirred up sentiments within that lay slumbering, and called into existence an entirely new train of thought. It was a new and special revelation, explaining dark and mysterious things, with which my youthful understanding had struggled, but struggled in vain. I now understood what had been to me a most perplexing difficulty—to wit, the white man's power to enslave the black man. It was a grand achievement, and I prized it highly. From that moment, I understood the pathway from slavery to freedom. It was just what I wanted, and I got it at a time when I the least expected it. Whilst I was saddened by the thought of losing the aid of my kind mistress, I was gladdened by the invaluable instruction which, by the merest accident, I had gained from my master. Though conscious of the difficulty of learning without a teacher, I set out with high hope, and a fixed purpose, at whatever cost of trouble, to learn how to read. The very decided manner with which he spoke, and strove to impress his wife with the evil consequences of giving me instruction, served to convince me that he was deeply sensible of the truths he was uttering. It gave me the best assurance that I might rely with the utmost confidence on the results which, he said, would flow from teaching me to read. What he most dreaded, that I most desired. What he most loved, that I most hated. That which to him was a great evil, to be carefully shunned, was to me a great good, to be diligently sought; and the argument which he so warmly urged, against my learning to read, only served to inspire me with a desire and determination to learn. In learning to read, I owe almost as much to the bitter opposition of my master, as to the kindly aid of my mistress. I acknowledge the benefit of both.

I had resided but a short time in Baltimore before I observed a marked difference, in the treatment of slaves, from that which I had witnessed in the country. A city slave is almost a freeman, compared with a slave on the plantation. He is much better fed and clothed, and enjoys privileges altogether unknown to the slave on the plantation. There is a vestige of decency, a sense of shame, that does much to curb and check those outbreaks of atrocious cruelty so commonly enacted upon the plantation. He is a desperate slaveholder, who will shock the humanity of his non-slaveholding neighbors with the cries of his lacerated slave. Few are willing to incur the odium attaching to the reputation of being a cruel master; and above all things, they would not be known as not giving a slave enough to eat. Every city slaveholder is anxious to have it known of him, that he feeds his slaves well; and it is due to them to say, that most of them do give their slaves enough to eat. There are, however, some painful exceptions to this rule. Directly opposite to us, on Philpot Street, lived Mr. Thomas Hamilton. He owned two slaves. Their names were Henrietta and Mary. Henrietta was about twenty-two years of age, Mary was about fourteen; and of all the mangled and emaciated creatures I ever looked upon, these two were the most so. His heart must be harder than stone, that could look upon these unmoved. The head, neck, and shoulders of Mary were literally cut to pieces. I have frequently felt her head, and found it nearly covered with festering sores, caused by the lash of her cruel mistress. I do not know that her master ever whipped her, but I have been an eye-witness to the cruelty of Mrs. Hamilton. I used to be in Mr. Hamilton's house nearly every day. Mrs. Hamilton used to sit in a large chair in the middle of the room, with a heavy cowskin always by her side, and scarce an hour passed during the day but was marked by the blood of one of these slaves. The girls seldom passed her without her saying, "Move faster, you *black gip!*" at the same time giving them a blow with a cowskin over the head or shoulders, often drawing the blood. She would then say, "Take that, you *black gip!*"— continuing, "If you don't move faster, I'll move you!" Added to the cruel lashings to which these slaves were subjected, they were kept nearly half-starved. They seldom knew what it was to eat a full meal. I have seen Mary contending with the pigs for the offal thrown into the street. So much was Mary kicked and cut to pieces, that she was oftener called *"pecked"* than by her name.

CHAPTER VII

I LIVED in Master Hugh's family about seven
years. During this time, I succeeded in learning to
read and write. In accomplishing this, I was compelled to resort to various stratagems. I had no regular
teacher. My mistress, who had kindly commenced to
instruct me, had, in compliance with the advice and
direction of her husband, not only ceased to instruct,
but had set her face against my being instructed by
any one else. It is due, however, to my mistress to say
of her, that she did not adopt this course of treatment
immediately. She at first lacked the depravity indispensable to shutting me up in mental darkness. It
was at least necessary for her to have some training in
the exercise of irresponsible power, to make her equal
to the task of treating me as though I were a brute.

My mistress was, as I have said, a kind and tender-hearted woman; and in the simplicity of her soul she commenced, when I first went to live with her, to treat me as she supposed one human being ought to treat another. In entering upon the duties of a slaveholder, she did not seem to perceive that I sustained to her the relation of a mere chattel, and that for her to treat me as a human being was not only wrong, but dangerously so. Slavery proved as injurious to her as it did to me. When I went there, she was a pious, warm, and tender-hearted woman. There was no sorrow or suffering for which she had not a tear. She had bread for the hungry, clothes for the naked, and comfort for every mourner that came within her reach. Slavery soon proved its ability to divest her of these heavenly qualities. Under its influence, the tender heart became stone, and the lamblike disposition gave way to one of tiger-like fierceness. The first step in her downward course was in her ceasing to instruct me. She now commenced to practise her husband's precepts. She finally became even more violent in her opposition than her husband himself. She was not satisfied with simply doing as well as he had commanded; she seemed anxious to do better. Nothing seemed to make her more angry than to see me with a newspaper. She seemed to think that here lay the danger. I have had her rush at me with a face made all up of fury, and snatch from me a newspaper, in a manner that fully revealed her apprehension. She was an apt woman; and a little experience soon demonstrated, to her satisfaction, that education and slavery were incompatible with each other.

From this time I was most narrowly watched. If I was in a separate room any considerable length of time, I was sure to be suspected of having a book, and was at once called to give an account of myself. All this, however, was too late. The first step had been taken. Mistress, in teaching me the alphabet, had given me the *inch,* and no precaution could prevent me from taking the *ell.*

The plan which I adopted, and the one by which I was most successful, was that of making friends of all the little white boys whom I met in the street. As many of these as I could, I converted into teachers. With their kindly aid, obtained at different times and in different places, I finally succeeded in learning to read. When I was sent of errands, I always took my book with me, and by going one part of my errand quickly, I found time to get a lesson before my return. I used also to carry bread with me, enough of which was always in the house, and to which I was always welcome; for I was much better off in this regard than many of the poor white children in our neighborhood. This bread I used to bestow upon the hungry little urchins, who, in return, would give me that more valuable bread of knowledge. I am strongly tempted to give the names of two or three of those little boys, as a testimonial of the gratitude and affection I bear them; but prudence forbids;—not that it would injure me, but it might embarrass them; for it is almost an unpardonable offence to teach slaves to read in this Christian country. It is enough to say of the dear little fellows, that they lived on Philpot Street, very near Durgin and Bailey's ship-yard. I used to talk this matter of slavery over with them. I would sometimes say to them, I wished I could be as free as they would be when they got to be men. "You will be free as soon as you are twenty-one, *but I am a slave for life*! Have not I as good a right to be free as you have?" These words used to trouble them; they would express for me the liveliest sympathy, and console me with the hope that something would occur by which I might be free.

I was now about twelve years old, and the thought of being *a slave for life* began to bear heavily upon my heart. Just about this time, I got hold of a book entitled "The Columbian Orator." Every opportunity I got, I used to read this book. Among much of other interesting matter, I found in it a dialogue between a master and his slave. The slave was represented as having run away from his master three times. The dialogue represented the conversation which took place between them, when the slave was retaken the third time. In this dialogue, the whole argument in behalf of slavery was brought forward by the master, all of which was disposed of by the slave. The slave was made to say some very smart as well as impressive things in reply to his master—things which had the desired though unexpected effect; for the conversation resulted in the voluntary emancipation of the slave on the part of the master.

In the same book, I met with one of Sheridan's mighty speeches on and in behalf of Catholic emancipation. These were choice documents to me. I read them over and over again with unabated interest. They gave tongue to interesting thoughts of my own soul, which had frequently flashed through my mind, and died away for want of utterance. The moral which I gained from the dialogue was the power of truth over the conscience of even a slaveholder. What I got from Sheridan was a bold denunciation of slavery, and a powerful vindication of human rights. The reading of these documents enabled me to utter my thoughts, and to meet the arguments brought forward to sustain slavery; but while they relieved me of one difficulty, they brought on another even more painful than the one of which I was relieved. The more I read, the more I was led to abhor and detest my enslavers. I could regard them in no other light than a band of successful robbers, who had left their homes, and gone to Africa, and stolen us from our homes, and in a strange land reduced us to slavery. I loathed them as being the meanest as well as the most wicked of men. As I read and contemplated the subject, behold! that very discontentment which Master Hugh had predicted would follow my learning to read had already come, to torment and sting my soul to unutterable anguish. As I writhed under it, I would at times feel that learning to read had been a curse rather than a blessing. It had given me a view of my wretched condition, without the remedy. It opened my eyes to the horrible pit, but to no ladder upon which to get out. In moments of agony, I envied my fellow-slaves for their stupidity. I have often wished myself a beast. I preferred the condition of the meanest reptile to my own. Any thing, no matter what, to get rid of thinking! It was this everlasting thinking of my condition that tormented me. There was no getting rid of it. It was pressed upon me by every object within sight or hearing, animate or inanimate. The silver trump of freedom had roused my soul to eternal wakefulness. Freedom now appeared, to disappear no more forever. It was heard in every sound, and seen in every thing. It was ever present to torment me with a sense of my wretched condition. I saw nothing without seeing it, I heard nothing without hearing it, and felt nothing without feeling it. It looked from every star, it smiled in every calm, breathed in every wind, and moved in every storm.

I often found myself regretting my own existence, and wishing myself dead; and but for the hope of being free, I have no doubt but that I should have killed myself, or done something for which I should have been killed. While in this state of mind, I was eager to hear any one speak of slavery. I was a ready listener. Every little while, I could hear something about the abolitionists. It was some time before I found what the word meant. It was always used in such connections as to make it an interesting word to me. If a slave ran away and succeeded in getting clear, or if a slave killed his master, set fire to a barn, or did any thing very wrong in the mind of a slaveholder, it was spoken of as the fruit of *abolition*. Hearing the word in this connection very often, I set about learning what it meant. The dictionary afforded me little or no help. I found it was "the act of abolishing;" but then I did not know what was to be abolished. Here I was perplexed. I did not dare to ask any one about its meaning, for I was satisfied that it was something they wanted me to know very little about. After a patient waiting, I got one of our city papers, containing an account of the number of petitions from the north, praying for the abolition of slavery in the District of Columbia, and of the slave trade between the States. From this time I understood the words *abolition* and *abolitionist,* and always drew near when that word was spoken, expecting to hear something of importance to myself and fellow-slaves. The light broke in upon me by degrees. I went one day down on the wharf of Mr. Waters; and seeing two Irishmen unloading a scow of stone, I went, unasked, and helped them. When we had finished, one of them came to me and asked me if I were a slave. I told him I was. He asked, "Are ye a slave for life?" I told him that I was. The good Irishman seemed to be deeply affected by the statement. He said to the other that it was a pity so fine a little fellow as myself should be a slave for life. He said it was a shame to hold me. They both advised me to run away to the north; that I should find friends there, and that I should be free. I pretended not to be interested in what they said, and treated them as if I did not understand them; for I feared they might be treacherous. White men have been known to encourage slaves to escape, and then, to get the reward, catch them and return them to their masters. I was afraid that these seemingly good men might use me so; but I nevertheless remembered their advice, and from that time I resolved to run away. I looked forward to a time at which it would be safe for me to escape. I was too young to think of doing so immediately; besides, I wished to learn how to write, as I might have occasion to write my own pass. I consoled myself with the hope that I should one day find a good chance. Meanwhile, I would learn to write.

The idea as to how I might learn to write was suggested to me by being in Durgin and Bailey's ship-yard, and frequently seeing the ship carpenters, after hewing, and getting a piece of timber ready for use, write on the timber the name of that part of the ship for which it was intended. When a piece of timber was intended for the larboard side, it would be marked thus—"L." When a piece was for the starboard side, it would be marked thus—"S." A piece of the larboard side forward, would be marked thus—"L. F." When a piece was for starboard side forward, it would be marked thus—"S. F." For larboard aft, it would be marked thus—"L. A." For starboard aft, it would be marked thus—"S. A." I soon learned the names of these letters, and for what they were intended when placed upon a piece of timber in the ship-yard. I immediately commenced copying them, and in a short time was able to make the four letters named. After that, when I met with any boy who I knew could write, I would tell him I could write as well as he. The next word would be, "I don't believe you. Let me see you try it." I would then make the letters which I had been so fortunate as to learn, and ask him to beat that. In this way I got a good many lessons in writing, which it is quite possible I should never have gotten in any other way. During this time, my copy-book was the board fence, brick wall, and pavement; my pen and ink was a lump of chalk. With these, I learned mainly how to write. I then commenced and continued copying the Italics in Webster's Spelling Book, until I could make them all without looking on the book. By this time, my little Master Thomas had gone to school, and learned how to write, and had written over a number of copy-books. These had been brought home, and shown to some of our near neighbors, and then laid aside. My mistress used to go to class meeting at the Wilk Street meetinghouse every Monday afternoon, and leave me to take care of the house. When left thus, I used to spend the time in writing in the spaces left in Master Thomas's copy-book, copying what he had written. I continued to do this until I could write a hand very similar to that of Master Thomas. Thus, after a long, tedious effort for years, I finally succeeded in learning how to write.

CHAPTER VIII

IN a very short time after I went to live at Baltimore, my old master's youngest son Richard died; and in about three years and six months after his death, my old master, Captain Anthony, died, leaving only his son, Andrew, and daughter, Lucretia, to share his estate. He died while on a visit to see his daughter at Hillsborough. Cut off thus unexpectedly, he left no will as to the disposal of his property. It was therefore necessary to have a valuation of the property, that it might be equally divided between Mrs. Lucretia and Master Andrew. I was immediately sent for, to be valued with the other property. Here again my feelings rose up in detestation of slavery. I had now a new conception of my degraded condition. Prior to this, I had become, if not insensible to my lot, at least partly so. I left Baltimore with a young heart overborne with sadness, and a soul full of apprehension. I took passage with Captain Rowe, in the schooner Wild Cat, and, after a sail of about twenty-four hours, I found myself near the place of my birth. I had now been absent from it almost, if not quite, five years. I, however, remembered the place very well. I was only about five years old when I left it, to go and live with my old master on Colonel Lloyd's plantation; so that I was now between ten and eleven years old.

We were all ranked together at the valuation. Men and women, old and young, married and single, were ranked with horses, sheep, and swine. There were horses and men, cattle and women, pigs and children, all holding the same rank in the scale of being, and were all subjected to the same narrow examination. Silvery-headed age and sprightly youth, maids and matrons, had to undergo the same indelicate inspection. At this moment, I saw more clearly than ever the brutalizing effects of slavery upon both slave and slaveholder.

After the valuation, then came the division. I have no language to express the high excitement and deep anxiety which were felt among us poor slaves during this time. Our fate for life was now to be decided. We had no more voice in that decision than the brutes among whom we were ranked. A single word from the white men was enough—against all our wishes, prayers, and entreaties—to sunder forever the dearest friends, dearest kindred, and strongest ties known to human beings. In addition to the pain of separation, there was the horrid dread of falling into the hands of Master Andrew. He was known to us all as being a most cruel wretch,—a common drunkard, who had, by his reckless mismanagement and profligate dissipation, already wasted a large portion of his father's property. We all felt that we might as well be sold at once to the Georgia traders, as to pass into his hands; for we knew that that would be our inevitable condition,—a condition held by us all in the utmost horror and dread.

I suffered more anxiety than most of my fellow-slaves. I had known what it was to be kindly treated; they had known nothing of the kind. They had seen little or nothing of the world. They were in very deed men and women of sorrow, and acquainted with grief. Their backs had been made familiar with the bloody lash, so that they had become callous; mine was yet tender; for while at Baltimore I got few whippings, and few slaves could boast of a kinder master and mistress than myself; and the thought of passing out of their hands into those of Master

Andrew—a man who, but a few days before, to give me a sample of his bloody disposition, took my little brother by the throat, threw him on the ground, and with the heel of his boot stamped upon his head till the blood gushed from his nose and ears—was well calculated to make me anxious as to my fate. After he had committed this savage outrage upon my brother, he turned to me, and said that was the way he meant to serve me one of these days,—meaning, I suppose, when I came into his possession.

Thanks to a kind Providence, I fell to the portion of Mrs. Lucretia, and was sent immediately back to Baltimore, to live again in the family of Master Hugh. Their joy at my return equalled their sorrow at my departure. It was a glad day to me. I had escaped a worse than lion's jaws. I was absent from Baltimore, for the purpose of valuation and division, just about one month, and it seemed to have been six.

Very soon after my return to Baltimore, my mistress, Lucretia, died, leaving her husband and one child, Amanda; and in a very short time after her death, Master Andrew died. Now all the property of my old master, slaves included, was in the hands of strangers,—strangers who had had nothing to do with accumulating it. Not a slave was left free. All remained slaves, from the youngest to the oldest. If any one thing in my experience, more than another, served to deepen my conviction of the infernal character of slavery, and to fill me with unutterable loathing of slaveholders, it was their base ingratitude to my poor old grandmother. She had served my old master faithfully from youth to old age. She had been the source of all his wealth; she had peopled his plantation with slaves; she had become a great grandmother in his service. She had rocked him in infancy, attended him in childhood, served him through life, and at his death wiped from his icy brow the cold death-sweat, and closed his eyes forever. She was nevertheless left a slave—a slave for life—a slave in the hands of strangers; and in their hands she saw her children, her grandchildren, and her great-grandchildren, divided, like so many sheep, without being gratified with the small privilege of a single word, as to their or her own destiny. And, to cap the climax of their base ingratitude and fiendish barbarity, my grandmother, who was now very old, having outlived my old master and all his children, having seen the beginning and end of all of them, and her present owners finding she was of but little value, her frame already racked with the pains of old age, and complete helplessness fast stealing over her once active limbs, they took her to the woods, built her a little hut, put up a little mud-chimney, and then made her welcome to the privilege of supporting herself there in perfect lone-liness; thus virtually turning her out to die! If my poor old grandmother now lives, she lives to suffer in utter loneliness; she lives to remember and mourn over the loss of children, the loss of grandchildren, and the loss of great-grandchildren. They are, in the language of the slave's poet, Whittier,—

"Gone, gone, sold and gone
To the rice swamp dank and lone,
Where the slave-whip ceaseless swings,
Where the noisome insect stings,
Where the fever-demon strews
Poison with the falling dews,
Where the sickly sunbeams glare
Through the hot and misty air:—
　　Gone, gone, sold and gone
　　To the rice swamp dank and lone,
　　From Virginia hills and waters—
　　Woe is me, my stolen daughters!"

The hearth is desolate. The children, the uncon-scious children, who once sang and danced in her presence, are gone. She gropes her way, in the dark-ness of age, for a drink of water. Instead of the voices of her children, she hears by day the moans of the dove, and by night the screams of the hideous owl.

All is gloom. The grave is at the door. And now, when weighed down by the pains and aches of old age, when the head inclines to the feet, when the beginning and ending of human existence meet, and helpless infancy and painful old age combine together—at this time, this most needful time, the time for the exercise of that tenderness and affection which children only can exercise towards a declining parent—my poor old grandmother, the devoted mother of twelve children, is left all alone, in yonder little hut, before a few dim embers. She stands—she sits—she staggers—she falls—she groans—she dies—and there are none of her children or grandchildren present, to wipe from her wrinkled brow the cold sweat of death, or to place beneath the sod her fallen remains. Will not a righteous God visit for these things?

In about two years after the death of Mrs. Lucretia, Master Thomas married his second wife. Her name was Rowena Hamilton. She was the eldest daughter of Mr. William Hamilton. Master now lived in St. Michael's. Not long after his marriage, a misunderstanding took place between himself and Master Hugh; and as a means of punishing his brother, he took me from him to live with himself at St. Michael's. Here I underwent another most painful separation. It, however, was not so severe as the one I dreaded at the division of property; for, during this interval, a great change had taken place in Master Hugh and his once kind and affectionate wife. The influence of brandy upon him, and of slavery upon her, had effected a disastrous change in the characters of both; so that, as far as they were concerned, I thought I had little to lose by the change. But it was not to them that I was attached. It was to those little Baltimore boys that I felt the strongest attachment. I had received many good lessons from them, and was still receiving them, and the thought of leaving them was painful indeed. I was leaving, too, without the hope of ever being allowed to return. Master Thomas had said he would never let me return again. The barrier betwixt himself and brother he considered impassable.

I then had to regret that I did not at least make the attempt to carry out my resolution to run away; for the chances of success are tenfold greater from the city than from the country.

I sailed from Baltimore for St. Michael's in the sloop Amanda, Captain Edward Dodson. On my passage, I paid particular attention to the direction which the steamboats took to go to Philadelphia. I found, instead of going down, on reaching North Point they went up the bay, in a north-easterly direction. I deemed this knowledge of the utmost importance. My determination to run away was again revived. I resolved to wait only so long as the offering of a favorable opportunity. When that came, I was determined to be off.

CHAPTER IX

I HAVE now reached a period of my life when I can give dates. I left Baltimore, and went to live with Master Thomas Auld, at St. Michael's, in March, 1832. It was now more than seven years since I lived with him in the family of my old master, on Colonel Lloyd's plantation. We of course were now almost entire strangers to each other. He was to me a new master, and I to him a new slave. I was ignorant of his temper and disposition; he was equally so of mine. A very short time, however, brought us into full acquaintance with each other. I was made acquainted with his wife not less than with himself. They were well matched, being equally mean and cruel. I was now, for the first time during a space of more than seven years, made to feel the painful gnawings of hunger—a something which I had not experienced before since I left Colonel Lloyd's plantation. It went hard enough with me then, when I could look back to no period at which I had enjoyed a sufficiency. It was tenfold harder after living in Master Hugh's family, where I had always had enough to eat, and of that which was good. I have said Master Thomas was a mean man. He was so. Not to give a slave enough to eat, is regarded as the most aggravated development of meanness even among slaveholders. The rule is, no matter how coarse the food, only let there be enough of it. This is the theory; and in the part of Maryland from which I came, it is the general practice,— though there are many exceptions. Master Thomas gave us enough of neither coarse nor fine food. There were four slaves of us in the kitchen—my sister Eliza, my aunt Priscilla, Henny, and myself; and we were allowed less than a half of a bushel of corn-meal per week, and very little else, either in the shape of meat or vegetables. It was not enough for us to subsist upon. We were therefore reduced to the wretched necessity of living at the expense of our neighbors. This we did by begging and stealing, whichever came handy in the time of need, the one being considered as legitimate as the other. A great many times have we poor creatures been nearly perishing with hunger, when food in abundance lay mouldering in the safe and smoke-house, and our pious mistress was aware of the fact; and yet that mistress and her husband would kneel every morning, and pray that God would bless them in basket and store!

Bad as all slaveholders are, we seldom meet one destitute of every element of character commanding respect. My master was one of this rare sort. I do not know of one single noble act ever performed by him. The leading trait in his character was meanness; and if there were any other element in his nature, it was made subject to this. He was mean; and, like most other mean men, he lacked the ability to conceal his meanness. Captain Auld was not born a slaveholder. He had been a poor man, master only of a Bay craft. He came into possession of all his slaves by marriage; and of all men, adopted slaveholders are the worst. He was cruel, but cowardly. He commanded without firmness. In the enforcement of his rules, he was at times rigid, and at times lax. At times, he spoke to his slaves with the firmness of Napoleon and the fury of a demon; at other times, he might well be mistaken for an inquirer who had lost his way. He did nothing of himself. He might have passed for a lion, but for his ears. In all things noble which he attempted, his own meanness shone most conspicuous.

His airs, words, and actions, were the airs, words, and actions of born slaveholders, and, being assumed, were awkward enough. He was not even a good imitator. He possessed all the disposition to deceive, but wanted the power. Having no resources within himself, he was compelled to be the copyist of many, and being such, he was forever the victim of inconsistency; and of consequence he was an object of contempt, and was held as such even by his slaves. The luxury of having slaves of his own to wait upon him was something new and unprepared for. He was a slaveholder without the ability to hold slaves. He found himself incapable of managing his slaves either by force, fear, or fraud. We seldom called him "master;" we generally called him "Captain Auld," and were hardly disposed to title him at all. I doubt not that our conduct had much to do with making him appear awkward, and of consequence fretful. Our want of reverence for him must have perplexed him greatly. He wished to have us call him master, but lacked the firmness necessary to command us to do so. His wife used to insist upon our calling him so, but to no purpose. In August, 1832, my master attended a Methodist camp-meeting held in the Bay-side, Talbot county, and there experienced religion. I indulged a faint hope that his conversion would lead him to emancipate his slaves, and that, if he did not do this, it would, at any rate, make him more kind and humane. I was disappointed in both these respects. It neither made him to be humane to his slaves, nor to emancipate them. If it had any effect on his character, it made him more cruel and hateful in all his ways; for I believe him to have been a much worse man after his conversion than before. Prior to his conversion, he relied upon his own depravity to shield and sustain him in his savage barbarity; but after his conversion, he found religious sanction and support for his slaveholding cruelty. He made the greatest pretensions to piety. His house was the house of prayer. He prayed morning, noon, and night. He very soon distinguished himself among his brethren, and was soon made a class-leader and exhorter. His activity in revivals was great, and he proved himself an instrument in the hands of the church in converting many souls. His house was the preachers' home. They used to take great pleasure in coming there to put up; for while he starved us, he stuffed them. We have had three or four preachers there at a time. The names of those who used to come most frequently while I lived there, were Mr. Storks, Mr. Ewery, Mr. Humphry, and Mr. Hickey. I have also seen Mr. George Cookman at our house. We slaves loved Mr. Cookman. We believed him to be a good man. We thought him instrumental in getting

Mr. Samuel Harrison, a very rich slaveholder, to emancipate his slaves; and by some means got the impression that he was laboring to effect the emancipation of all the slaves. When he was at our house, we were sure to be called in to prayers. When the others were there, we were sometimes called in and sometimes not. Mr. Cookman took more notice of us than either of the other ministers. He could not come among us without betraying his sympathy for us, and, stupid as we were, we had the sagacity to see it.

While I lived with my master in St. Michael's, there was a white young man, a Mr. Wilson, who proposed to keep a Sabbath school for the instruction of such slaves as might be disposed to learn to read the New Testament. We met but three times, when Mr. West and Mr. Fairbanks, both class-leaders, with many others, came upon us with sticks and other missiles, drove us off, and forbade us to meet again. Thus ended our little Sabbath school in the pious town of St. Michael's.

I have said my master found religious sanction for his cruelty. As an example, I will state one of many facts going to prove the charge. I have seen him tie up a lame young woman, and whip her with a heavy cowskin upon her naked shoulders, causing the warm red blood to drip; and, in justification of the bloody deed, he would quote this passage of Scripture—"He that knoweth his master's will, and doeth it not, shall be beaten with many stripes."

Master would keep this lacerated young woman tied up in this horrid situation four or five hours at a time. I have known him to tie her up early in the morning, and whip her before breakfast; leave her, go to his store, return at dinner, and whip her again, cutting her in the places already made raw with his cruel lash. The secret of master's cruelty toward "Henny" is found in the fact of her being almost helpless. When quite a child, she fell into the fire, and burned herself horribly. Her hands were so burnt that she never got the use of them. She could do very little but bear heavy burdens. She was to master a bill of expense; and as he was a mean man, she was a constant offence to him. He seemed desirous of getting the poor girl out of existence. He gave her away once to his sister; but, being a poor gift, she was not disposed to keep her. Finally, my benevolent master, to use his own words, "set her adrift to take care of herself." Here was a recently-converted man, holding on upon the mother, and at the same time turning out her helpless child, to starve and die! Master Thomas was one of the many pious slaveholders who hold slaves for the very charitable purpose of taking care of them.

My master and myself had quite a number of differences. He found me unsuitable to his purpose. My city life, he said, had had a very pernicious effect upon me. It had almost ruined me for every good purpose, and fitted me for every thing which was bad. One of my greatest faults was that of letting his horse run away, and go down to his father-in-law's farm, which was about five miles from St. Michael's. I would then have to go after it. My reason for this kind of carelessness, or carefulness, was, that I could always get something to eat when I went there. Master William Hamilton, my master's father-in-law, always gave his slaves enough to eat. I never left there hungry, no matter how great the need of my speedy return. Master Thomas at length said he would stand it no longer. I had lived with him nine months, during which time he had given me a number of severe whippings, all to no good purpose. He resolved to put me out, as he said, to be broken; and, for this purpose, he let me for one year to a man named Edward Covey. Mr. Covey was a poor man, a farm-renter. He rented the place upon which he lived, as also the hands with which he tilled it. Mr. Covey had acquired a very high reputation for breaking young slaves, and this reputation was of immense value to him. It enabled him to get his farm tilled with much less expense to himself than he could have had it done without such a reputation. Some slaveholders thought it not much loss to allow Mr. Covey to have their slaves one year, for the sake of the training to which they were subjected, without any other compensation. He could hire young help with great ease, in consequence of this reputation. Added to the natural good qualities of Mr. Covey, he was a professor of religion—a pious soul—a member and a class-leader in the Methodist church. All of this added weight to his reputation as a "nigger-breaker." I was aware of all the facts, having been made acquainted with them by a young man who had lived there. I nevertheless made the change gladly; for I was sure of getting enough to eat, which is not the smallest consideration to a hungry man.

CHAPTER X

I LEFT Master Thomas's house, and went to live with Mr. Covey, on the 1st of January, 1833. I was now, for the first time in my life, a field hand. In my new employment, I found myself even more awkward than a country boy appeared to be in a large city. I had been at my new home but one week before Mr. Covey gave me a very severe whipping, cutting my back, causing the blood to run, and raising ridges on my flesh as large as my little finger. The details of this affair are as follows: Mr. Covey sent me, very early in the morning of one of our coldest days in the month of January, to the woods, to get a load of wood. He gave me a team of unbroken oxen. He told me which was the in-hand ox, and which the off-hand one. He then tied the end of a large rope around the horns of the in-hand ox, and gave me the other end of it, and told me, if the oxen started to run, that I must hold on upon the rope. I had never driven oxen before, and of course I was very awkward. I, however, succeeded in getting to the edge of the woods with little difficulty; but I had got a very few rods into the woods, when the oxen took fright, and started full tilt, carrying the cart against trees, and over stumps, in the most frightful manner. I expected every moment that my brains would be dashed out against the trees. After running thus for a considerable distance, they finally upset the cart, dashing it with great force against a tree, and threw themselves into a dense thicket. How I escaped death, I do not know. There I was, entirely alone, in a thick wood, in a place new to me. My cart was upset and shattered, my oxen were entangled among the young trees, and there was none to help me. After a long spell of effort, I succeeded in getting my cart righted, my oxen disentangled, and again yoked to the cart. I now proceeded with my team to the place where I had, the day before, been chopping wood, and loaded my cart pretty heavily, thinking in this way to tame my oxen. I then proceeded on my way home. I had now consumed one half of the day. I got out of the woods safely, and now felt out of danger. I stopped my oxen to open the woods gate; and just as I did so, before I could get hold of my ox-rope, the oxen again started, rushed through the gate, catching it between the wheel and the body of the cart, tearing it to pieces, and coming within a few inches of crushing me against the gate-post. Thus twice, in one short day, I escaped death by the merest chance. On my return, I told Mr. Covey what had happened, and how it happened. He ordered me to return to the woods again immediately. I did so, and he followed on after me. Just as I got into the woods, he came up and told me to stop my cart, and that he would teach me how to trifle away my time, and break gates. He then went to a large gum-tree, and with his axe cut three large switches, and, after trimming them up neatly with his pocket-knife, he ordered me to take off my clothes. I made him no answer, but stood with my clothes on. He repeated his order. I still made him no answer, nor did I move to strip myself. Upon this he rushed at me with the fierceness of a tiger, tore off my clothes, and lashed me till he had worn out his switches, cutting me so savagely as to leave the marks visible for a long time after. This whipping was the first of a number just like it, and for similar offences.

I lived with Mr. Covey one year. During the first six months, of that year, scarce a week passed without his whipping me. I was seldom free from a sore back. My awkwardness was almost always his excuse for whipping me. We were worked fully up to the point of endurance. Long before day we were up, our horses fed, and by the first approach of day we were off to the field with our hoes and ploughing teams. Mr. Covey gave us enough to eat, but scarce time to eat it. We were often less than five minutes taking our meals. We were often in the field from the first approach of day till its last lingering ray had left us; and at saving-fodder time, midnight often caught us in the field binding blades.

Covey would be out with us. The way he used to stand it, was this. He would spend the most of his afternoons in bed. He would then come out fresh in the evening, ready to urge us on with his words, example, and frequently with the whip. Mr. Covey was one of the few slaveholders who could and did work with his hands. He was a hard-working man. He knew by himself just what a man or a boy could do. There was no deceiving him. His work went on in his absence almost as well as in his presence; and he had the faculty of making us feel that he was ever present with us. This he did by surprising us. He seldom approached the spot where we were at work openly, if he could do it secretly. He always aimed at taking us by surprise. Such was his cunning, that we used to call him, among ourselves, "the snake."

When we were at work in the cornfield, he would sometimes crawl on his hands and knees to avoid detection, and all at once he would rise nearly in our midst, and scream out, "Ha, ha! Come, come! Dash on, dash on!" This being his mode of attack, it was never safe to stop a single minute. His comings were like a thief in the night. He appeared to us as being ever at hand. He was under every tree, behind every stump, in every bush, and at every window, on the plantation. He would sometimes mount his horse, as if bound to St. Michael's, a distance of seven miles, and in half an hour afterwards you would see him coiled up in the corner of the wood-fence, watching every motion of the slaves. He would, for this purpose, leave his horse tied up in the woods. Again, he would sometimes walk up to us, and give us orders as though he was upon the point of starting on a long journey, turn his back upon us, and make as though he was going to the house to get ready; and, before he would get half way thither, he would turn short and crawl into a fence-corner, or behind some tree, and there watch us till the going down of the sun.

Mr. Covey's *forte* consisted in his power to deceive. His life was devoted to planning and perpetrating the grossest deceptions. Every thing he possessed in the shape of learning or religion, he made conform to his disposition to deceive. He seemed to think himself equal to deceiving the Almighty. He would make a short prayer in the morning, and a long prayer at night; and, strange as it may seem, few men would at times appear more devotional than he. The exercises of his family devotions were always commenced with singing; and, as he was a very poor singer himself, the duty of raising the hymn generally came upon me. He would read his hymn, and nod at me to commence. I would at times do so; at others, I would not. My non-compliance would almost always produce much confusion. To show himself independent of me, he would start and stagger through with his hymn in the most discordant manner. In this state of mind, he prayed with more than ordinary spirit. Poor man! such was his disposition, and success at deceiving, I do verily believe that he sometimes deceived himself into the solemn belief, that he was a sincere worshipper of the most high God; and this, too, at a time when he may be said to have been guilty of compelling his woman slave to commit the sin of adultery. The facts in the case are these: Mr. Covey was a poor man; he was just commencing in life; he was only able to buy one slave; and, shocking as is the fact, he bought her, as he said, for *a breeder.* This woman was named Caroline. Mr. Covey bought her from Mr. Thomas

Lowe, about six miles from St. Michael's. She was a large, able-bodied woman, about twenty years old. She had already given birth to one child, which proved her to be just what he wanted. After buying her, he hired a married man of Mr. Samuel Harrison, to live with him one year; and him he used to fasten up with her every night! The result was, that, at the end of the year, the miserable woman gave birth to twins. At this result Mr. Covey seemed to be highly pleased, both with the man and the wretched woman. Such was his joy, and that of his wife, that nothing they could do for Caroline during her confinement was too good, or too hard, to be done. The children were regarded as being quite an addition to his wealth.

If at any one time of my life more than another, I was made to drink the bitterest dregs of slavery, that time was during the first six months of my stay with Mr. Covey. We were worked in all weathers. It was never too hot or too cold; it could never rain, blow, hail, or snow, too hard for us to work in the field. Work, work, work, was scarcely more the order of the day than of the night. The longest days were too short for him, and the shortest nights too long for him. I was somewhat unmanageable when I first went there, but a few months of this discipline tamed me. Mr. Covey succeeded in breaking me.

I was broken in body, soul, and spirit. My natural elasticity was crushed, my intellect languished, the disposition to read departed, the cheerful spark that lingered about my eye died; the dark night of slavery closed in upon me; and behold a man transformed into a brute!

Sunday was my only leisure time. I spent this in a sort of beast-like stupor, between sleep and wake, under some large tree. At times I would rise up, a flash of energetic freedom would dart through my soul, accompanied with a faint beam of hope, that flickered for a moment, and then vanished. I sank down again, mourning over my wretched condition. I was sometimes prompted to take my life, and that of Covey, but was prevented by a combination of hope and fear. My sufferings on this plantation seem now like a dream rather than a stern reality.

Our house stood within a few rods of the Chesapeake Bay, whose broad bosom was ever white with sails from every quarter of the habitable globe. Those beautiful vessels, robed in purest white, so delightful to the eye of freemen, were to me so many shrouded ghosts, to terrify and torment me with thoughts of my wretched condition. I have often, in the deep stillness of a summer's Sabbath, stood all alone upon the lofty banks of that noble bay, and traced, with saddened heart and tearful eye, the countless number of sails moving off to the mighty ocean. The sight of these always affected me powerfully. My thoughts would compel utterance; and there, with no audience but the Almighty, I would pour out my soul's complaint, in my rude way, with an apostrophe to the moving multitude of ships:—

"You are loosed from your moorings, and are free; I am fast in my chains, and am a slave! You move merrily before the gentle gale, and I sadly before the bloody whip! You are freedom's swift-winged angels that fly round the world; I am confined in bands of iron! O that I were free! O, that I were on one of your gallant decks, and under your protecting wing! Alas! betwixt me and you, the turbid waters roll. Go on, go on. O that I could also go! Could I but swim! If I could fly! O, why was I born a man, of whom to make a brute! The glad ship is gone; she hides in the dim distance. I am left in the hottest hell of unending slavery. O God, save me! God, deliver me! Let me be free! Is there any God? Why am I a slave? I will run away. I will not stand it. Get caught, or get clear, I'll try it. I had as well die with ague as the fever. I have only one life to lose. I had as well be killed running as die standing. Only think of it; one hundred miles straight north, and I am free! Try it? Yes! God helping me, I will. It cannot be that I shall live and die a slave. I will take to

the water. This very bay shall yet bear me into freedom. The steamboats steered in a north-east course
from North Point. I will do the same; and when I
get to the head of the bay, I will turn my canoe
adrift, and walk straight through Delaware into
Pennsylvania. When I get there, I shall not be
required to have a pass; I can travel without being
disturbed. Let but the first opportunity offer, and,
come what will, I am off. Meanwhile, I will try to
bear up under the yoke. I am not the only slave in
the world. Why should I fret? I can bear as much as
any of them. Besides, I am but a boy, and all boys are
bound to some one. It may be that my misery in
slavery will only increase my happiness when I get
free. There is a better day coming."

Thus I used to think, and thus I used to speak
to myself; goaded almost to madness at one moment, and at the next reconciling myself to my
wretched lot.

I have already intimated that my condition was
much worse, during the first six months of my stay
at Mr. Covey's, than in the last six. The circumstances leading to the change in Mr. Covey's course
toward me form an epoch in my humble history. You
have seen how a man was made a slave; you shall see
how a slave was made a man. On one of the hottest
days of the month of August, 1833, Bill Smith,

William Hughes, a slave named Eli, and myself, were engaged in fanning wheat. Hughes was clearing the fanned wheat from before the fan. Eli was turning, Smith was feeding, and I was carrying wheat to the fan. The work was simple, requiring strength rather than intellect; yet, to one entirely unused to such work, it came very hard. About three o'clock of that day, I broke down; my strength failed me; I was seized with a violent aching of the head, attended with extreme dizziness; I trembled in every limb. Finding what was coming, I nerved myself up, feeling it would never do to stop work. I stood as long as I could stagger to the hopper with grain. When I could stand no longer, I fell, and felt as if held down by an immense weight. The fan of course stopped; every one had his own work to do; and no one could do the work of the other, and have his own go on at the same time.

Mr. Covey was at the house, about one hundred yards from the treading-yard where we were fanning. On hearing the fan stop, he left immediately, and came to the spot where we were. He hastily inquired what the matter was. Bill answered that I was sick, and there was no one to bring wheat to the fan. I had by this time crawled away under the side of the post and rail-fence by which the yard was enclosed, hoping to find relief by getting out of the sun. He then asked where I was. He was told by one of the hands. He came to the spot, and, after looking at me awhile, asked me what was the matter. I told him as well as I could, for I scarce had strength to speak. He then gave me a savage kick in the side, and told me to get up. I tried to do so, but fell back in the attempt. He gave me another kick, and again told me to rise. I again tried, and succeeded in gaining my feet; but, stooping to get the tub with which I was feeding the fan, I again staggered and fell. While down in this situation, Mr. Covey took up the hickory slat with which Hughes had been striking off the half-bushel measure, and with it gave me a heavy blow upon the head, making a large wound, and the blood ran freely; and with this again told me to get up. I made no effort to comply, having now made up my mind to let him do his worst. In a short time after receiving this blow, my head grew better. Mr. Covey had now left me to my fate. At this moment I resolved, for the first time, to go to my master, enter a complaint, and ask his protection. In order to do this, I must that afternoon walk seven miles; and this, under the circumstances, was truly a severe undertaking. I was exceedingly feeble; made so as much by the kicks and blows which I received, as by the severe fit of sickness to which I had been subjected. I, however, watched my chance, while Covey was looking in an opposite direction, and started for St. Michael's. I succeeded in getting a considerable distance on my way to the woods, when Covey discovered me, and called after me to come back, threatening what he would do if I did not come. I disregarded both his calls and his threats, and made my way to the woods as fast as my feeble state would allow; and thinking I might be overhauled by him if I kept the road, I walked through the woods, keeping far enough from the road to avoid detection, and near enough to prevent losing my way. I had not gone far before my little strength again failed me. I could go no farther. I fell down, and lay for a considerable time. The blood was yet oozing from the wound on my head. For a time I thought I should bleed to death; and think now that I should have done so, but that the blood so matted my hair as to stop the wound. After lying there about three quarters of an hour, I nerved myself up again, and started on my way, through bogs and briers, barefooted and bareheaded, tearing my feet sometimes at nearly every step; and after a journey of about seven miles, occupying some five hours to perform it, I arrived at master's store. I then presented an appearance enough to affect any but a heart of iron. From the crown of my head to my feet, I was covered with blood. My hair was all clotted with dust and blood;

my shirt was stiff with blood. My legs and feet were torn in sundry places with briers and thorns, and were also covered with blood. I suppose I looked like a man who had escaped a den of wild beasts, and barely escaped them. In this state I appeared before my master, humbly entreating him to interpose his authority for my protection. I told him all the circumstances as well as I could, and it seemed, as I spoke, at times to affect him. He would then walk the floor, and seek to justify Covey by saying he expected I deserved it. He asked me what I wanted. I told him, to let me get a new home; that as sure as I lived with Mr. Covey again, I should live with but to die with him; that Covey would surely kill me; he was in a fair way for it. Master Thomas ridiculed the idea that there was any danger of Mr. Covey's killing me, and said that he knew Mr. Covey; that he was a good man, and that he could not think of taking me from him; that, should he do so, he would lose the whole year's wages; that I belonged to Mr. Covey for one year, and that I must go back to him, come what might; and that I must not trouble him with any more stories, or that he would himself *get hold of me.* After threatening me thus, he gave me a very large dose of salts, telling me that I might remain in St. Michael's that night, (it being quite late,) but that I must be off back to Mr. Covey's early in the morning; and that if I did not, he would *get hold of me,* which meant that he would whip me. I remained all night, and, according to his orders, I started off to Covey's in the morning, (Saturday morning,) wearied in body and broken in spirit. I got no supper that night, or breakfast that morning. I reached Covey's about nine o'clock; and just as I was getting over the fence that divided Mrs. Kemp's fields from ours, out ran Covey with his cowskin, to give me another whipping. Before he could reach me, I succeeded in getting to the cornfield; and as the corn was very high, it afforded me the means of hiding. He seemed very angry, and searched for me a long time. My behavior was altogether unaccountable. He finally gave up the chase, thinking I suppose, that I must come home for something to eat; he would give himself no further trouble in looking for me. I spent that day mostly in the woods, having the alternative before me,—to go home and be whipped to death, or stay in the woods and be starved to death. That night, I fell in with Sandy Jenkins, a slave with whom I was somewhat acquainted. Sandy had a free wife who lived about four miles from Mr. Covey's; and it being Saturday, he was on his way to see her. I told him my circumstances, and he very kindly invited me to go home with him. I went home with him, and talked this whole matter over, and got his advice as to what course it was best for me to pursue. I found Sandy an old adviser. He told me, with great solemnity, I must go back to Covey; but that before I went, I must go with him into another part of the woods, where there was a certain *root,* which, if I would take some of it with me, carrying it *always on my right side,* would render it impossible for Mr. Covey, or any other white man, to whip me. He said he had carried it for years; and since he had done so, he had never received a blow, and never expected to while he carried it. I at first rejected the idea, that the simple carrying of a root in my pocket would have any such effect as he had said, and was not disposed to take it; but Sandy impressed the necessity with much earnestness, telling me it could do no harm, if it did no good. To please him, I at length took the root, and, according to his direction, carried it upon my right side. This was Sunday morning. I immediately started for home; and upon entering the yard gate, out came Mr. Covey on his way to meeting. He spoke to me very kindly, bade me drive the pigs from a lot near by, and passed on towards the church. Now, this singular conduct of Mr. Covey really made me begin to think that there was something in the *root* which Sandy had given me; and had it been on any other day than Sunday, I could have attributed the conduct to no other cause than the influence of that root; and as it was, I was half inclined to think the *root* to be something more than I at first had taken it to be. All went well till Monday morning. On this morning, the virtue of the *root* was fully tested. Long before daylight, I was called to go and rub, curry, and feed, the horses. I obeyed, and was glad to obey. But whilst thus engaged, whilst in the act of throwing down some blades from the loft, Mr. Covey entered the stable with a long rope; and just as I was half out of the loft, he caught hold of my legs, and was about tying me. As soon as I found what he was up to, I gave a sudden spring, and as I did so, he holding to my legs, I was brought sprawling on the stable floor. Mr. Covey seemed now to think he had me, and could do what he pleased; but at this moment— from whence came the spirit I don't know—I resolved to fight; and, suiting my action to the reso- lution, I seized Covey hard by the throat; and as I did so, I rose. He held on to me, and I to him. My resist- ance was so entirely unexpected, that Covey seemed taken all aback. He trembled like a leaf. This gave me assurance, and I held him uneasy, causing the blood to run where I touched him with the ends of my fingers. Mr. Covey soon called out to Hughes for help. Hughes came, and, while Covey held me, attempted to tie my right hand. While he was in the act of doing so, I watched my chance, and gave him a heavy kick close under the ribs. This kick fairly sickened Hughes, so that he left me in the hands of Mr. Covey. This kick had the effect of not only weakening Hughes, but Covey also. When he saw Hughes bending over with pain, his courage quailed. He asked me if I meant to persist in my resistance. I told him I did, come what might; that he had used me like a brute for six months, and that I was determined to be used so no longer. With that, he strove to drag me to a stick that was lying just out of the stable door. He meant to knock me down. But just as he was leaning over to get the stick, I seized him with both hands by his collar, and brought him by a sudden snatch to the ground. By this time, Bill came. Covey called upon him for assistance. Bill wanted to know what he could do. Covey said, "Take hold of him, take hold of him!" Bill said his master hired him out to work, and not to help to whip me; so he left Covey and myself to fight our own battle out. We were at it for nearly two hours. Covey at length let me go, puffing and blowing at a great rate, saying that if I had not resisted, he would not have whipped me half so much. The truth was, that he had not whipped me at all. I considered him as getting entirely the worst end of the bargain; for he had drawn no blood from me, but I had from him.

The whole six months afterwards, that I spent with Mr. Covey, he never laid the weight of his finger upon me in anger. He would occasionally say, he didn't want to get hold of me again. "No," thought I, "you need not; for you will come off worse than you did before."

This battle with Mr. Covey was the turning-point in my career as a slave. It rekindled the few expiring embers of freedom, and revived within me a sense of my own manhood. It recalled the departed self-confidence, and inspired me again with a determination to be free. The gratification afforded by the triumph was a full compensation for whatever else might follow, even death itself. He only can understand the deep satisfaction which I experienced, who has himself repelled by force the bloody arm of slavery. I felt as I never felt before. It was a glorious resurrection, from the tomb of slavery, to the heaven of freedom. My long-crushed spirit rose, cowardice departed, bold defiance took its place; and I now resolved that, however long I might remain a slave in form, the day had passed forever when I could be a slave in fact. I did not hesitate to let it be known of me, that the white man who expected to succeed in whipping, must also succeed in killing me.

From this time I was never again what might be called fairly whipped, though I remained a slave four years afterward. I had several fights, but was never whipped.

It was for a long time a matter of surprise to me why Mr. Covey did not immediately have me taken by the constable to the whipping-post, and there regularly whipped for the crime of raising my hand against a white man in defence of myself. And the only explanation I can now think of does not entirely satisfy me; but such as it is, I will give it. Mr. Covey enjoyed the most unbounded reputation for being a first-rate overseer and negro-breaker. It was of considerable importance to him. That reputation was at stake; and had he sent me—a boy about sixteen years old—to the public whipping-post, his reputation would have been lost; so, to save his reputation, he suffered me to go unpunished.

My term of actual service to Mr. Edward Covey ended on Christmas day, 1833. The days between Christmas and New Year's day are allowed as holidays; and, accordingly, we were not required to perform any labor, more than to feed and take care of the stock. This time we regarded as our own, by the grace of our masters; and we therefore used or abused it nearly as we pleased. Those of us who had families at a distance, were generally allowed to spend the whole six days in their society. This time, however, was spent in various ways. The staid, sober, thinking and industrious ones of our number would employ themselves in making corn-brooms, mats, horse-collars, and baskets; and another class of us would spend the time in hunting opossums, hares, and coons. But by far the larger part engaged in such sports and merriments as playing ball, wrestling, running foot-races, fiddling, dancing, and drinking whisky; and this latter mode of spending the time was by far the most agreeable to the feelings of our masters. A slave who would work during the holidays was considered by our masters as scarcely deserving them. He was regarded as one who rejected the favor of his master. It was deemed a disgrace not to get drunk at Christmas; and he was regarded as lazy indeed, who had not provided himself with the necessary means, during the year, to get whisky enough to last him through Christmas.

From what I know of the effect of these holidays upon the slave, I believe them to be among the most effective means in the hands of the slaveholder in keeping down the spirit of insurrection. Were the slaveholders at once to abandon this practice, I have not the slightest doubt it would lead to an immediate insurrection among the slaves. These holidays serve as conductors, or safety-valves, to carry off the rebellious spirit of enslaved humanity. But for these, the slave would be forced up to the wildest

95

desperation; and woe betide the slaveholder, the day he ventures to remove or hinder the operation of those conductors! I warn him that, in such an event, a spirit will go forth in their midst, more to be dreaded than the most appalling earthquake.

The holidays are part and parcel of the gross fraud, wrong, and inhumanity of slavery. They are professedly a custom established by the benevolence of the slaveholders; but I undertake to say, it is the result of selfishness, and one of the grossest frauds committed upon the down-trodden slave. They do not give the slaves this time because they would not like to have their work during its continuance, but because they know it would be unsafe to deprive them of it. This will be seen by the fact, that the slaveholders like to have their slaves spend those days just in such a manner as to make them as glad of their ending as of their beginning. Their object seems to be, to disgust their slaves with freedom, by plunging them into the lowest depths of dissipation. For instance, the slaveholders not only like to see the slave drink of his own accord, but will adopt various plans to make him drunk. One plan is, to make bets on their slaves, as to who can drink the most whisky without getting drunk; and in this way they succeed in getting whole multitudes to drink to excess. Thus, when the slave asks for virtuous freedom, the cunning slaveholder, knowing his ignorance, cheats him with a dose of vicious dissipation, artfully labelled with the name of liberty. The most of us used to drink it down, and the result was just what might be supposed: many of us were led to think that there was little to choose between liberty and slavery. We felt, and very properly too, that we had almost as well be slaves to man as to rum. So, when the holidays ended, we staggered up from the filth of our wallowing, took a long breath, and marched to the field,—feeling, upon the whole, rather glad to go, from what our master had deceived us into a belief was freedom, back to the arms of slavery.

I have said that this mode of treatment is a part of the whole system of fraud and inhumanity of slavery. It is so. The mode here adopted to disgust the slave with freedom, by allowing him to see only the abuse of it, is carried out in other things. For instance, a slave loves molasses; he steals some. His master, in many cases, goes off to town, and buys a large quantity; he returns, takes his whip, and commands the slave to eat the molasses, until the poor fellow is made sick at the very mention of it. The same mode is sometimes adopted to make the slaves refrain from asking for more food than their regular allowance. A slave runs through his allowance, and applies for more. His master is enraged at him; but, not willing to send him off without food, gives him more than is necessary, and compels him to eat it within a given time. Then, if he complains that he cannot eat it, he is said to be satisfied neither full nor fasting, and is whipped for being hard to please! I have an abundance of such illustrations of the same principle, drawn from my own observation, but think the cases I have cited sufficient. The practice is a very common one.

On the first of January, 1834, I left Mr. Covey, and went to live with Mr. William Freeland, who lived about three miles from St. Michael's. I soon found Mr. Freeland a very different man from Mr. Covey. Though not rich, he was what would be called an educated southern gentleman. Mr. Covey, as I have shown, was a well-trained negro-breaker and slave-driver. The former (slaveholder though he was) seemed to possess some regard for honor, some reverence for justice, and some respect for humanity. The latter seemed totally insensible to all such sentiments. Mr. Freeland had many of the faults peculiar to slaveholders, such as being very passionate and fretful; but I must do him the justice to say, that he was exceedingly free from those degrading vices to which Mr. Covey was constantly addicted. The one was open and frank, and we always knew where to find him. The other was a most artful deceiver, and could be understood only by such as were skilful enough to detect his cunningly-devised frauds. Another advantage I gained in my new master was, he made no pretensions to, or profession of, religion; and this, in my opinion, was truly a great advantage. I assert most unhesitatingly, that the religion of the south is a mere covering for the most horrid crimes,—a justifier of the most appalling bar- barity,—a sanctifier of the most hateful frauds,— and a dark shelter under, which the darkest, foulest, grossest, and most infernal deeds of slaveholders find the strongest protection. Were I to be again reduced to the chains of slavery, next to that enslavement, I should regard being the slave of a religious master the greatest calamity that could befall me. For of all slaveholders with whom I have ever met, religious slaveholders are the worst. I have ever found them the meanest and basest, the most cruel and cowardly, of all others. It was my unhappy lot not only to be- long to a religious slaveholder, but to live in a com- munity of such religionists. Very near Mr. Freeland lived the Rev. Daniel Weeden, and in the same neighborhood lived the Rev. Rigby Hopkins. These were members and ministers in the Reformed Methodist Church. Mr. Weeden owned, among others, a woman slave, whose name I have forgotten. This woman's back, for weeks, was kept literally raw, made so by the lash of this merciless, *religious* wretch. He used to hire hands. His maxim was, Behave well or behave ill, it is the duty of a master occasionally to whip a slave, to remind him of his master's authority. Such was his theory, and such his practice.

Mr. Hopkins was even worse than Mr. Weeden. His chief boast was his ability to manage slaves. The peculiar feature of his government was that of whipping slaves in advance of deserving it. He always managed to have one or more of his slaves to whip every Monday morning. He did this to alarm their fears, and strike terror into those who escaped. His plan was to whip for the smallest offences, to prevent the commission of large ones. Mr. Hopkins could always find some excuse for whipping a slave. It would astonish one, unaccustomed to a slave-holding life, to see with what wonderful ease a slaveholder can find things, of which to make occasion to whip a slave. A mere look, word, or motion,—a mistake, accident, or want of power,—are all matters for which a slave may be whipped at any time. Does a slave look dissatisfied? It is said, he has the devil in him, and it must be whipped out. Does he speak loudly when spoken to by his master? Then he is getting high-minded, and should be taken down a button-hole lower. Does he forget to pull off his hat at the approach of a white person? Then he is wanting in reverence, and should be whipped for it. Does he ever venture to vindicate his conduct, when censured for it? Then he is guilty of impudence,— one of the greatest crimes of which a slave can be guilty. Does he ever venture to suggest a different mode of doing things from that pointed out by his master? He is indeed presumptuous, and getting above himself; and nothing less than a flogging will do for him. Does he, while ploughing, break a plough,—or, while hoeing, break a hoe? It is owing to his carelessness, and for it a slave must always be whipped. Mr. Hopkins could always find something of this sort to justify the use of the lash, and he seldom failed to embrace such opportunities. There was not a man in the whole county, with whom the slaves who had the getting their own home, would not prefer to live, rather than with this Rev. Mr. Hopkins. And yet there was not a man any where round, who made higher professions of religion, or was more active in revivals,—more attentive to the class, love-feast, prayer and preaching meetings, or more devotional in his family,—that prayed earlier, later, louder, and longer,—than this same reverend slave-driver, Rigby Hopkins.

But to return to Mr. Freeland, and to my experience while in his employment. He, like Mr. Covey, gave us enough to eat; but, unlike Mr. Covey, he also gave us sufficient time to take our meals. He worked us hard, but always between sunrise and sunset. He required a good deal of work to be done, but gave us good tools with which to work. His farm was large, but he employed hands enough to work it, and with ease, compared with many of his neighbors. My treatment, while in his employment, was heavenly, compared with what I experienced at the hands of Mr. Edward Covey.

Mr. Freeland was himself the owner of but two slaves. Their names were Henry Harris and John Harris. The rest of his hands he hired. These consisted of myself, Sandy Jenkins,[1] and Handy Caldwell. Henry and John were quite intelligent, and in a very little while after I went there, I succeeded in creating in them a strong desire to learn how to read. This desire soon sprang up in the others also. They very soon mustered up some old spelling-books, and nothing would do but that I must keep a Sabbath school. I agreed to do so, and accordingly devoted my Sundays to teaching these my loved fellow-slaves how to read. Neither of them knew his letters when I went there. Some of the slaves of the

---

1. This is the same man who gave me the roots to prevent my being whipped by Mr. Covey. He was "a clever soul." We used frequently to talk about the fight with Covey, and as often as we did so, he would claim my success as the result of the roots which he gave me. This superstition is very common among the more ignorant slaves. A slave seldom dies but that his death is attributed to trickery.

neighboring farms found what was going on, and also availed themselves of this little opportunity to learn to read. It was understood, among all who came, that there must be as little display about it as possible. It was necessary to keep our religious masters at St. Michael's unacquainted with the fact, that, instead of spending the Sabbath in wrestling, boxing, and drinking whisky, we were trying to learn how to read the will of God; for they had much rather see us engaged in those degrading sports, then to see us behaving like intellectual, moral, and accountable beings. My blood boils as I think of the bloody manner in which Messrs. Wright Fairbanks and Garrison West, both class-leaders, in connection with many others, rushed in upon us with sticks and stones, and broke up our virtuous little Sabbath school, at St. Michael's—all calling themselves Christians! humble followers of the Lord Jesus Christ! But I am again digressing.

I held my Sabbath school at the house of a free colored man, whose name I deem it imprudent to mention; for should it be known, it might embarrass him greatly, though the crime of holding the school was committed ten years ago. I had at one time over forty scholars, and those of the right sort, ardently desiring to learn. They were of all ages, though mostly men and women. I look back to those

Sundays with an amount of pleasure not to be expressed. They were great days to my soul. The work of instructing my dear fellow-slaves was the sweetest engagement with which I was ever blessed. We loved each other, and to leave them at the close of the Sabbath was a severe cross indeed. When I think that these precious souls are to-day shut up in the prison-house of slavery, my feelings overcome me, and I am almost ready to ask, "Does a righteous God govern the universe? and for what does he hold the thunders in his right hand, if not to smite the oppressor, and deliver the spoiled out of the hand of the spoiler?" These dear souls came not to Sabbath school because it was popular to do so, nor did I teach them because it was reputable to be thus engaged. Every moment they spent in that school, they were liable to be taken up, and given thirty-nine lashes. They came because they wished to learn. Their minds had been starved by their cruel masters. They had been shut up in mental darkness. I taught them, because it was the delight of my soul to be doing something that looked like bettering the conditions of my race. I kept up my school nearly the whole year I lived with Mr. Freeland; and, beside my Sabbath school, I devoted three evenings in the week, during the winter, to teaching the slaves at home. And I have the happiness to know, that several of those who came to Sabbath school learned how to read; and that one, at least, is now free through my agency.

The year passed off smoothly. It seemed only about half as long as the year which preceded it. I went through it without receiving a single blow. I will give Mr. Freeland the credit of being the best master I ever had, *till I became my own master.* For the ease with which I passed the year, I was, however, somewhat indebted to the society of my fellow-slaves. They were noble souls; they not only possessed loving hearts, but brave ones. We were linked and interlinked with each other. I loved them with a love stronger than any thing I have experienced since. It is sometimes said that we slaves do not love and confide in each other. In answer to this assertion, I can say, I never loved any or confided in any people more than my fellow-slaves, and especially those with whom I lived at Mr. Freeland's. I believe we would have died for each other. We never undertook to do any thing, of any importance, without a mutual consultation. We never moved separately. We were one; and as much so by our tempers and dispositions, as by the mutual hardships to which we were necessarily subjected by our condition as slaves.

At the close of the year 1834, Mr. Freeland again hired me of my master, for the year 1835. But, by this time, I began to want to live *upon free land* as well as *with Freeland;* and I was no longer content, therefore, to live with him or any other slaveholder. I began, with the commencement of the year, to prepare myself for a final struggle, which should decide my fate one way or the other. My tendency was upward. I was fast approaching manhood, and year after year had passed, and I was still a slave. These thoughts roused me—I must do something. I therefore resolved that 1835 should not pass without witnessing an attempt, on my part, to secure my liberty. But I was not willing to cherish this determination alone. My fellow-slaves were dear to me. I was anxious to have them participate with me in this, my life-giving determination. I therefore, though with great prudence, commenced early to ascertain their views and feelings in regard to their condition, and to imbue their minds with thoughts of freedom. I bent myself to devising ways and means for our escape, and meanwhile strove, on all fitting occasions, to impress them with the gross fraud and inhumanity of slavery. I went first to Henry, next to John, then to the others. I found, in them all, warm hearts and noble spirits. They were ready to hear, and ready to act when a feasible plan should be proposed. This was what I wanted. I talked to them of our want of manhood, if we submitted to our enslavement without at least one noble effort to be free. We met often, and consulted frequently, and told our hopes and fears, recounted the difficulties, real and imagined, which we should be called on to meet. At times we were almost disposed to give up, and try to content ourselves with our wretched lot; at others, we were firm and unbending in our determination to go. Whenever we suggested any plan, there was shrinking—the odds were fearful. Our path was beset with the greatest obstacles; and if we succeeded in gaining the end of it, our right to be free was yet questionable—we were yet liable to be returned to bondage. We could see no spot, this side of the ocean, where we could be free. We knew nothing about Canada. Our knowledge of the north did not extend farther than New York; and to go there, and be forever harassed with the frightful liability of being returned to slavery—with the certainty of being treated tenfold worse than before—the thought was truly a horrible one, and one which it was not easy to overcome. The case sometimes stood thus: At every gate through which we were to pass, we saw a watchman—at every ferry a guard—on every bridge a sentinel—and in every wood a patrol. We were hemmed in upon every side. Here were the difficulties, real or imagined—the good to be sought, and the evil to be shunned. On the one hand, there stood slavery, a stern reality, glaring frightfully upon us,—its robes already crimsoned with the blood of millions, and even now feasting itself greedily upon our own flesh. On the other hand, away back in the dim distance, under the flickering light of the north star, behind some craggy hill or snow-covered mountain, stood a doubtful freedom—half frozen—beckoning us to come and share its hospitality. This in itself was sometimes enough to stagger us; but when we permitted ourselves to survey the road, we were frequently appalled. Upon either side we saw grim death, assuming the most horrid shapes. Now it was starvation, causing us to eat our own flesh;—now we were contending with the waves, and were drowned;—now we were overtaken, and torn to pieces by the fangs of the terrible bloodhound. We were stung by scorpions, chased by wild beasts, bitten by snakes, and finally, after having nearly reached the desired spot,—after swimming rivers, encountering wild beasts, sleeping in the woods, suffering hunger and nakedness,—we were overtaken by our pursuers, and, in our resistance, we were shot dead upon the spot! I say, this picture sometimes appalled us, and made us

"rather bear those ills we had,
Than fly to others, that we knew not of."

In coming to a fixed determination to run away, we did more than Patrick Henry, when he resolved upon liberty or death. With us it was a doubtful liberty at most, and almost certain death if we failed. For my part, I should prefer death to hopeless bondage.

Sandy, one of our number, gave up the notion, but still encouraged us. Our company then consisted of Henry Harris, John Harris, Henry Bailey, Charles Roberts, and myself. Henry Bailey was my uncle, and belonged to my master. Charles married my aunt: he belonged to my master's father-in-law, Mr. William Hamilton.

The plan we finally concluded upon was, to get a large canoe belonging to Mr. Hamilton, and upon the Saturday night previous to Easter holidays, paddle directly up the Chesapeake Bay. On our arrival at the head of the bay, a distance of seventy or eighty miles from where we lived, it was our purpose to turn our canoe adrift, and follow the guidance of the north star till we got beyond the limits of Maryland. Our reason for taking the water route was, that we were less liable to be suspected as runaways; we hoped to be regarded as fishermen; whereas, if we should take the land route, we should be subjected to interruptions of almost every kind. Any one having a white face, and being so disposed, could stop us, and subject us to examination.

The week before our intended start, I wrote several protections, one for each of us. As well as I can remember, they were in the following words, to wit:—

"This is to certify that I, the undersigned, have given the bearer, my servant, full liberty to go to Baltimore, and spend the Easter holidays. Written with mine own hand, &c., 1835.

"WILLIAM HAMILTON,
"Near St. Michael's, in Talbot county, Maryland."

We were not going to Baltimore; but, in going up the bay, we went toward Baltimore, and these protections were only intended to protect us while on the bay.

As the time drew near for our departure, our anxiety became more and more intense. It was truly a matter of life and death with us. The strength of our determination was about to be fully tested. At this time, I was very active in explaining every difficulty, removing every doubt, dispelling every fear, and inspiring all with the firmness indispensable to success in our undertaking; assuring them that half was gained the instant we made the move; we had talked long enough; we were now ready to move; if not now, we never should be; and if we did not intend to move now, we had as well fold our arms, sit down, and acknowledge ourselves fit only to be slaves. This, none of us were prepared to acknowledge. Every man stood firm; and at our last meeting, we pledged ourselves afresh, in the most solemn manner, that, at the time appointed, we would certainly start in pursuit of freedom. This was in the middle of the week, at the end of which we were to be off. We went, as usual, to our several fields of labor, but with bosoms highly agitated with thoughts of our truly hazardous undertaking. We tried to conceal our feelings as much as possible; and I think we succeeded very well.

After a painful waiting, the Saturday morning, whose night was to witness our departure, came. I hailed it with joy, bring what of sadness it might. Friday night was a sleepless one for me. I probably felt more anxious than the rest, because I was, by common consent, at the head of the whole affair. The responsibility of success or failure lay heavily upon me. The glory of the one, and the confusion of the other, were alike mine. The first two hours of that morning were such as I never experienced before, and hope never to again. Early in the morning, we went, as usual, to the field. We were spreading manure; and all at once, while thus engaged, I was overwhelmed with an indescribable feeling, in the fulness of which I turned to Sandy, who was near by, and said, "We are betrayed!" "Well," said he, "that thought has this moment struck me." We said no more. I was never more certain of any thing.

The horn was blown as usual, and we went up from the field to the house for breakfast. I went for the form, more than for want of any thing to eat that morning. Just as I got to the house, in looking out at the lane gate, I saw four white men, with two colored men. The white men were on horseback, and the colored ones were walking behind, as if tied. I watched them a few moments till they got up to our lane gate. Here they halted, and tied the colored men to the gate-post. I was not yet certain as to what the matter was. In a few moments, in rode Mr. Hamilton, with a speed betokening great excitement. He came to the door, and inquired if Master William was in. He was told he was at the barn. Mr. Hamilton, without dismounting, rode up to the barn with extraordinary speed. In a few moments, he and Mr. Freeland returned to the house. By this time, the three constables rode up, and in great haste dismounted, tied their horses, and met Master William and Mr. Hamilton returning from the barn; and after talking awhile, they all walked up to the kitchen door. There was no one in the kitchen but myself and John. Henry and Sandy were up at the barn. Mr. Freeland put his head in at the door, and called me by name, saying, there were some gentlemen at the door who wished to see me. I stepped to the door, and inquired what they wanted. They at once seized me, and, without giving me any satisfaction, tied me—lashing my hands closely together. I insisted upon knowing what the matter was. They at length said, that they had learned I had been in a "scrape," and that I was to be examined before my master; and if their information proved false, I should not be hurt.

In a few moments, they succeeded in tying John. They then turned to Henry, who had by this time returned, and commanded him to cross his hands. "I won't!" said Henry, in a firm tone, indicating his readiness to meet the consequences of his refusal. "Won't you?" said Tom Graham, the constable. "No, I won't!" said Henry, in a still stronger tone. With this, two of the constables pulled out their shining pistols, and swore, by their Creator, that they would make him cross his hands or kill him. Each cocked his pistol, and, with fingers on the trigger, walked up to Henry, saying, at the same time, if he did not cross his hands, they would blow his damned heart out. "Shoot me, shoot me!" said Henry; "you can't kill me but once. Shoot, shoot,—and be damned! *I won't be tied!*" This he said in a tone of loud defiance; and at the same time, with a motion as quick as lightning, he with one single stroke dashed the pistols from the hand of each constable. As he did this, all hands fell upon him, and, after beating him some time, they finally overpowered him, and got him tied.

During the scuffle, I managed, I know not how, to get my pass out, and, without being discovered, put it into the fire. We were all now tied; and just as we were to leave for Easton jail, Betsy Freeland, mother of William Freeland, came to the door with her hands full of biscuits, and divided them between Henry and John. She then delivered herself of a speech, to the following effect:—addressing herself to me, she said, *"You devil! You yellow devil!* it was you that put it into the heads of Henry and John to run away. But for you, you long-legged mulatto devil! Henry nor John would never have thought of such a thing." I made no reply, and was immediately hurried off towards St. Michael's. Just a moment previous to the scuffle with Henry, Mr. Hamilton suggested the propriety of making a search for the protections which he had understood Frederick had written for himself and the rest. But, just at the moment he was about carrying his proposal into effect, his aid was needed in helping to tie Henry; and the excitement attending the scuffle caused them either to forget, or to deem it unsafe, under the circumstances, to search. So we were not yet convicted of the intention to run away.

When we got about halfway to St. Michael's, while the constables having us in charge were looking ahead, Henry inquired of me what he should do with his pass. I told him to eat it with his biscuit, and own nothing; and we passed the word around, *"Own nothing;"* and *"Own nothing!"* said we all. Our confidence in each other was unshaken. We were resolved to succeed or fail together, after the calamity had befallen us as much as before. We were now prepared for any thing. We were to be dragged that morning fifteen miles behind horses, and then to be placed in the Easton jail. When we reached St. Michael's, we underwent a sort of examination. We all denied that we ever intended to run away. We did this more to bring out the evidence against us, than from any hope of getting clear of being sold; for, as I have said, we were ready for that. The fact was, we cared but little where we went, so we went together. Our greatest concern was about separation. We dreaded that more than any thing this side of death. We found the evidence against us to be the testimony of one person; our master would not tell who it was; but we came to a unanimous decision among ourselves as to who their informant was. We were sent off to the jail at Easton. When we got there, we were delivered up to the sheriff, Mr. Joseph Graham, and by him placed in jail. Henry, John, and myself, were placed in one room together—Charles, and Henry Bailey, in another. Their object in separating us was to hinder concert.

We had been in jail scarcely twenty minutes, when a swarm of slave traders, and agents for slave traders, flocked into jail to look at us, and to ascertain if we were for sale. Such a set of beings I never saw before! I felt myself surrounded by so many fiends from perdition. A band of pirates never looked more like their father, the devil. They laughed and grinned over us, saying, "Ah, my boys! we have got you, haven't we?" And after taunting us in various ways, they one by one went into an examination of us, with intent to ascertain our value. They would impudently ask us if we would not like to have them for our masters. We would make them no answer, and leave them to find out as best they could. Then they would curse and swear at us, telling us that they could take the devil out of us in a very little while, if we were only in their hands.

While in jail, we found ourselves in much more comfortable quarters than we expected when we went there. We did not get much to eat, nor that which was very good; but we had a good clean room, from the windows of which we could see what was going on in the street, which was very much better than though we had been placed in one of the dark, damp cells. Upon the whole, we got along very well, so far as the jail and its keeper were concerned. Immediately after the holidays were over, contrary to all our expectations, Mr. Hamilton and Mr. Freeland came up to Easton, and took Charles, the two Henrys, and John, out of jail, and carried them home, leaving me alone. I regarded this separation as a final one. It caused me more pain than any thing else in the whole transaction. I was ready for any thing rather than separation. I supposed that they had consulted together, and had decided that, as I was the whole cause of the intention of the others to run away, it was hard to make the innocent suffer with the guilty; and that they had, therefore, concluded to take the others home, and sell me, as a warning to the others that remained. It is due to the noble Henry to say, he seemed almost as reluctant at leaving the prison as at leaving home to come to the prison. But we knew we should, in all probability, be separate, if we were sold; and since he was in their hands, he concluded to go peaceably home.

I was now left to my fate. I was all alone, and within the walls of a stone prison. But a few days before, and I was full of hope. I expected to have been safe in a land of freedom; but now I was covered with gloom, sunk down to the utmost despair. I thought the possibility of freedom was gone. I was kept in this way about one week, at the end of which, Captain Auld, my master, to my surprise and utter astonishment, came up, and took me out, with the intention of sending me, with a gentleman of his acquaintance, into Alabama. But, from some cause or other, he did not send me to Alabama, but concluded to send me back to Baltimore, to live again with his brother Hugh, and to learn a trade.

Thus, after an absence of three years and one month, I was once more permitted to return to my old home at Baltimore. My master sent me away, because there existed against me a very great prejudice in the community, and he feared I might be killed.

In a few weeks after I went to Baltimore, Master Hugh hired me to Mr. William Gardner, an extensive shipbuilder, on Fell's Point. I was put there to learn how to calk. It, however, proved a very unfavorable place for the accomplishment of this object. Mr. Gardner was engaged that spring in building two large man-of-war brigs, professedly for the Mexican government. The vessels were to be launched in the July of that year, and in failure thereof, Mr. Gardner was to lose a considerable sum; so that when I entered, all was hurry. There was no time to learn any thing. Every man had to do that which he knew how to do. In entering the shipyard, my orders from Mr. Gardner were, to do whatever the carpenters commanded me to do. This was placing me at the beck and call of about seventy-five men. I was to regard all these as masters. Their word was to be my law. My situation was a most trying one. At times I needed a dozen pair of hands. I was called a dozen ways in the space of a single minute. Three or four voices would strike my ear at the same moment. It was—"Fred., come help me to cant this timber here."—"Fred., come carry this timber yonder."—"Fred., bring that roller here."—"Fred., go get a fresh can of water."—"Fred., come help saw off the end of this timber."—"Fred., go quick, and get the crowbar."—"Fred., hold on the end of this fall."—"Fred., go to the blacksmith's shop, and get a new punch."—"Hurra, Fred.! run and bring me a cold chisel."—"I say, Fred., bear a hand, and get up a fire as quick as lightning under that steam-box."—"Halloo, nigger! come, turn this grindstone."—"Come, come! move, move! and *bowse* this timber forward."—"I say, darky, blast your eyes, why don't you heat up some pitch?"—"Halloo! halloo! halloo!" (Three voices at the same time.) "Come here!—Go there!—Hold on where you are! Damn you, if you move, I'll knock your brains out!"

This was my school for eight months; and I might have remained there longer, but for a most horrid fight I had with four of the white apprentices, in which my left eye was nearly knocked out, and I was horribly mangled in other respects. The facts in the case were these: Until a very little while after I went there, white and black ship-carpenters worked side by side, and no one seemed to see any impropriety in it. All hands seemed to be very well satisfied. Many of the black carpenters were freemen. Things seemed to be going on very well. All at once, the white carpenters knocked off, and said they would not work with free colored workmen. Their reason for this, as alleged, was, that if free colored carpenters were encouraged, they would soon take the trade into their own hands, and poor white men would be thrown out of employment. They therefore felt called upon at once to put a stop to it. And, taking advantage of Mr. Gardner's necessities, they broke off, swearing they would work no longer, unless he would discharge his black carpenters. Now, though this did not extend to me in form, it did reach me in fact. My fellow-apprentices very soon began to feel it degrading to them to work with me. They began to put on airs, and talk about the "niggers" taking the country, saying we all ought to be killed; and, being encouraged by the journeymen, they commenced making my condition as hard as they could, by hectoring me around, and sometimes striking me. I, of course, kept the vow I made after the fight with Mr. Covey, and struck back again, regardless of consequences; and while I kept them from combining, I succeeded very well; for I could whip the whole of them, taking them separately. They, however, at length combined, and came upon me, armed with sticks, stones, and heavy hand-spikes. One came in front with a half brick. There was one at each side of me, and one behind me. While I was attending to those in front, and on either side, the one behind ran up with the hand-spike, and struck me a heavy blow upon the head. It stunned me. I fell, and with this they all ran upon me, and fell to beating me with their fists. I let them lay on for a while, gathering strength. In an instant, I gave a sudden surge, and rose to my hands and knees. Just as I did that, one of their number gave me, with his heavy boot, a powerful kick in the left eye. My eyeball seemed to have burst. When they saw my eye closed, and badly swollen, they left me. With this I seized the handspike, and for a time pursued them. But here the carpenters interfered, and I thought I might as well give it up. It was impossible to stand my hand against so many. All this took place in sight of not less than fifty white ship-carpenters and not one interposed a friendly word; but some cried, "Kill the damned nigger! Kill him! kill him! He struck a white person." I found my only chance for life was in flight. I succeeded in getting away without an additional blow, and barely so; for to strike a white man is death by Lynch law,— and that was the law in Mr. Gardner's ship-yard; nor is there much of any other out of Mr. Gardner's ship-yard.

I went directly home, and told the story of my wrongs to Master Hugh; and I am happy to say of him, irreligious as he was, his conduct was heavenly, compared with that of his brother Thomas under similar circumstances. He listened attentively to my narration of the circumstances leading to the savage outrage, and gave many proofs of his strong indignation at it. The heart of my once overkind mistress was again melted into pity. My puffed-out eye and blood-covered face moved her to tears. She took a chair by me, washed the blood from my face, and, with a mother's tenderness, bound up my head, covering the wounded eye with a lean piece of fresh beef. It was almost compensation for my suffering to witness, once more, a manifestation of kindness from this, my once affectionate old mistress. Master Hugh was very much enraged. He gave expression to his feelings by pouring out curses upon the heads of those who did the deed. As soon as I got a little the better of my bruises, he took me with him to Esquire Watson's, on Bond Street, to see what could be done about the matter. Mr. Watson inquired who saw the assault committed. Master Hugh told him it was done in Mr. Gardner's ship-yard, at midday, where there were a large company of men at work. "As to that," he said, "the deed was done, and there was no question as to who did it." His answer was, he could do nothing in the case, unless some white man would come forward and testify. He could issue no warrant on my word. If I had been killed in the presence of a thousand colored people, their testimony combined would have been insufficient to have arrested one of the murderers. Master Hugh, for once, was compelled to say this state of things was too bad. Of course, it was impossible to get any white man to volunteer his testimony in my behalf, and against the white young men. Even those who may have sympathized with me were not prepared to do this. It required a degree of courage unknown to them to do so; for just at that time, the slightest manifestation of humanity toward a colored person was denounced as abolitionism, and that name subjected its bearer to frightful liabilities. The watchwords of the bloody-minded in that region, and in those days, were, "Damn the abolitionists!" and

"Damn the niggers!" There was nothing done, and probably nothing would have been done if I had been killed. Such was, and such remains, the state of things in the Christian city of Baltimore.

Master Hugh, finding he could get no redress, refused to let me go back again to Mr. Gardner. He kept me himself, and his wife dressed my wound till I was again restored to health. He then took me into the ship-yard of which he was foreman, in the employment of Mr. Walter Price. There I was immediately set to calking, and very soon learned the art of using my mallet and irons. In the course of one year from the time I left Mr. Gardner's, I was able to command the highest wages given to the most experienced calkers. I was now of some importance to my master. I was bringing him from six to seven dollars per week. I sometimes brought him nine dollars per week: my wages were a dollar and a half a day. After learning how to calk, I sought my own employment, made my own contracts, and collected the money which I earned. My pathway became much more smooth than before; my condition was now much more comfortable. When I could get no calking to do, I did nothing. During these leisure times, those old notions about freedom would steal over me again. When in Mr. Gardner's employment, I was kept in such a perpetual whirl of excitement, I could think of nothing, scarcely, but my life; and in thinking of my life, I almost forgot my liberty. I have observed this in my experience of slavery,—that whenever my condition was improved, instead of its increasing my contentment, it only increased my desire to be free, and set me to thinking of plans to gain my freedom. I have found that, to make a contented slave, it is necessary to make a thoughtless one. It is necessary to darken his moral and mental vision, and, as far as possible, to annihilate the power of reason. He must be able to detect no inconsistencies in slavery; he must be made to feel that slavery is right; and he can be brought to that only when he ceases to be a man.

I was now getting, as I have said, one dollar and fifty cents per day. I contracted for it; I earned it; it was paid to me; it was rightfully my own; yet, upon each returning Saturday night, I was compelled to deliver every cent of that money to Master Hugh. And why? Not because he earned it,—not because he had any hand in earning it,—not because I owed it to him,—nor because he possessed the slightest shadow of a right to it; but solely because he had the power to compel me to give it up. The right of the grim-visaged pirate upon the high seas is exactly the same.

CHAPTER XI

I NOW come to that part of my life during which I planned, and finally succeeded in making, my escape from slavery. But before narrating any of the peculiar circumstances, I deem it proper to make known my intention not to state all the facts connected with the transaction. My reasons for pursuing this course may be understood from the following: First, were I to give a minute statement of all the facts, it is not only possible, but quite probable, that others would thereby be involved in the most embarrassing difficulties. Secondly, such a statement would most undoubtedly induce greater vigilance on the part of the slaveholders than has existed heretofore among them; which would, of course, be the means of guarding a door whereby some dear brother bondman might escape his galling chains. I deeply regret the necessity that impels me to suppress any thing of importance connected with my experience in slavery. It would afford me great pleasure indeed, as well as materially add to the interest of my narrative, were I at liberty to gratify a curiosity, which I know exists in the minds of many, by an accurate statement of all the facts pertaining to my most fortunate escape. But I must deprive myself of this pleasure, and the curious of the gratification which such a statement would afford. I would allow myself to suffer under the greatest imputations which evil-minded men might suggest, rather than exculpate myself, and thereby run the hazard of closing the slightest avenue by which a brother slave might clear himself of the chains and fetters of slavery.

I have never approved of the very public manner in which some of our western friends have conducted what they call the *underground railroad,* but which I think, by their open declarations, has been made most emphatically the *upperground railroad.* I honor those good men and women for their noble daring, and applaud them for willingly subjecting themselves to bloody persecution, by openly avowing their participation in the escape of slaves. I, however, can see very little good resulting from such a course, either to themselves or the slaves escaping; while, upon the other hand, I see and feel assured that those open declarations are a positive evil to the slaves remaining, who are seeking to escape. They do nothing towards enlightening the slave, whilst they do much towards enlightening the master. They stimulate him to greater watchfulness, and enhance his power to capture his slave. We owe something to the slave south of the line as well as to those north of it; and in aiding the latter on their way to freedom, we should be careful to do nothing which would be likely to hinder the former from escaping from slavery. I would keep the merciless slaveholder profoundly ignorant of the means of flight adopted by the slave. I would leave him to imagine himself surrounded by myriads of invisible tormentors, ever ready to snatch from his infernal grasp his trembling prey. Let him be left to feel his way in the dark; let darkness commensurate with his crime hover over him; and let him feel that at every step he takes, in pursuit of the flying bondman, he is running the frightful risk of having his hot brains dashed out by an invisible agency. Let us render the tyrant no aid; let us not hold the light by which he can trace the footprints of our flying brother. But enough of this. I will now proceed to the statement of those facts, connected with my escape, for which I am alone responsible, and for which no one can be made to suffer but myself.

In the early part of the year 1838, I became quite restless. I could see no reason why I should, at the end of each week, pour the reward of my toil into the purse of my master. When I carried to him my weekly wages, he would, after counting the money, look me in the face with a robber-like fierceness, and ask, "Is this all?" He was satisfied with nothing less than the last cent. He would, however, when I made him six dollars, sometimes give me six cents, to encourage me. It had the opposite effect. I regarded it as a sort of admission of my right to the whole. The fact that he gave me any part of my wages was proof, to my mind, that he believed me entitled to the whole of them. I always felt worse for having received any thing; for I feared that the giving me a few cents would ease his conscience, and make him feel himself to be a pretty honorable sort of robber. My discontent grew upon me. I was ever on the look-out for means of escape; and, finding no direct means, I determined to try to hire my time, with a view of getting money with which to make my escape. In the spring of 1838, when Master Thomas came to Baltimore to purchase his spring goods, I got an opportunity, and applied to him to allow me to hire my time. He unhesitatingly refused my request, and told me this was another stratagem by which to escape. He told me I could go nowhere but that he could get me; and that, in the event of my running away, he should spare no pains in his efforts to catch me. He exhorted me to content myself, and be obedient. He told me, if I would be happy, I must lay out no plans for the future. He said, if I behaved myself properly, he would take care of me. Indeed, he advised me to complete thoughtlessness of the future, and taught me to depend solely upon him for happiness. He seemed to see fully the pressing necessity of setting aside my intellectual nature, in order to contentment in slavery. But in spite of him, and even in spite of myself, I continued to think, and to think about the injustice of my enslavement, and the means of escape.

About two months after this, I applied to Master Hugh for the privilege of hiring my time. He was not acquainted with the fact that I had applied to Master Thomas, and had been refused. He too, at first, seemed disposed to refuse; but, after some reflection, he granted me the privilege, and proposed the following terms: I was to be allowed all my time, make all contracts with those for whom I worked, and find my own employment; and, in return for this liberty, I was to pay him three dollars at the end of each week; find myself in calking tools, and in board and clothing. My board was two dollars and a half per week. This, with the wear and tear of clothing and calking tools, made my regular expenses about six dollars per week. This amount I was compelled to make up, or relinquish the privilege of hiring my time. Rain or shine, work or no work, at the end of each week the money must be forthcoming, or I must give up my privilege. This arrangement, it will be perceived, was decidedly in my master's favor. It relieved him of all need of looking after me. His money was sure. He received all the benefits of slave-holding without its evils; while I endured all the evils of a slave, and suffered all the care and anxiety of a freeman. I found it a hard bargain. But, hard as it was, I thought it better than the old mode of getting along. It was a step towards freedom to be allowed to bear the responsibilities of a freeman, and I was determined to hold on upon it. I bent myself to the work of making money. I was ready to work at night as well as day, and by the most untiring perseverance and industry, I made enough to meet my expenses, and lay up a little money every week. I went on thus from May till August. Master Hugh then refused to allow me to hire my time longer. The ground for his refusal was a failure on my part, one Saturday night, to pay him for my week's time. This failure was occasioned by my attending a camp meeting about

ten miles from Baltimore. During the week, I had
entered into an engagement with a number of young
friends to start from Baltimore to the camp ground
early Saturday evening; and being detained by my
employer, I was unable to get down to Master
Hugh's without disappointing the company. I knew
that Master Hugh was in no special need of the
money that night. I therefore decided to go to camp
meeting, and upon my return pay him the three
dollars. I staid at the camp meeting one day longer
than I intended when I left. But as soon as I
returned, I called upon him to pay him what he
considered his due. I found him very angry; he could
scarce restrain his wrath. He said he had a great
mind to give me a severe whipping. He wished to
know how I dared go out of the city without asking
his permission. I told him I hired my time, and
while I paid him the price which he asked for it, I
did not know that I was bound to ask him when
and where I should go. This reply troubled him; and,
after reflecting a few moments, he turned to me, and
said I should hire my time no longer; that the next
thing he should know of, I would be running away.
Upon the same plea, he told me to bring my tools
and clothing home forthwith. I did so; but instead of
seeking work, as I had been accustomed to do previously to hiring my time, I spent the whole week

without the performance of a single stroke of work. I did this in retaliation. Saturday night, he called upon me as usual for my week's wages. I told him I had no wages; I had done no work that week. Here we were upon the point of coming to blows. He raved, and swore his determination to get hold of me. I did not allow myself a single word; but was resolved, if he laid the weight of his hand upon me, it should be blow for blow. He did not strike me, but told me that he would find me in constant employ-ment in future. I thought the matter over during the next day, Sunday, and finally resolved upon the third day of September, as the day upon which I would make a second attempt to secure my freedom. I now had three weeks during which to prepare for my journey. Early on Monday morning, before Master Hugh had time to make an engagement for me, I went out and got employment of Mr. Butler, at his ship-yard near the drawbridge, upon what is called the City Block, thus making it unnecessary for him to seek employment for me. At the end of the week, I brought him between eight and nine dollars. He seemed very well pleased, and asked why I did not do the same the week before. He little knew what my plans were. My object in working steadily was to remove any suspicion he might entertain of my intent to run away; and in this I succeeded admirably.

I suppose he thought I was never better satisfied with my condition than at the very time during which I was planning my escape. The second week passed, and again I carried him my full wages; and so well pleased was he, that he gave me twenty-five cents, (quite a large sum for a slaveholder to give a slave,) and bade me to make a good use of it. I told him I would.

Things went on without very smoothly indeed, but within there was trouble. It is impossible for me to describe my feelings as the time of my contemplated start drew near. I had a number of warm-hearted friends in Baltimore,—friends that I loved almost as I did my life,—and the thought of being separated from them forever was painful beyond expression. It is my opinion that thousands would escape from slavery, who now remain, but for the strong cords of affection that bind them to their friends. The thought of leaving my friends was decidedly the most painful thought with which I had to contend. The love of them was my tender point, and shook my decision more than all things else. Beside the pain of separation, the dread and apprehension of a failure exceeded what I had experienced at my first attempt. The appalling defeat I then sustained returned to torment me. I felt assured that, if I failed in this attempt, my case would be a hopeless one—it would seal my fate as a slave forever. I could not hope to get off with any thing less than the severest punishment, and being placed beyond the means of escape. It required no very vivid imagination to depict the most frightful scenes through which I should have to pass, in case I failed. The wretchedness of slavery, and the blessedness of freedom, were perpetually before me. It was life and death with me. But I remained firm, and, according to my resolution, on the third day of September, 1838, I left my chains, and succeeded in reaching New York without the slightest interruption of any kind. How I did so,—what means I adopted,— what direction I travelled, and by what mode of conveyance,—I must leave unexplained, for the reasons before mentioned.

I have been frequently asked how I felt when I found myself in a free State. I have never been able to answer the question with any satisfaction to myself. It was a moment of the highest excitement I ever experienced. I suppose I felt as one may imagine the unarmed mariner to feel when he is rescued by a friendly man-of-war from the pursuit of a pirate. In writing to a dear friend, immediately after my arrival at New York, I said I felt like one who had escaped a den of hungry lions. This state of mind, however, very soon subsided; and I was again seized with a feeling of great insecurity and loneliness. I was yet liable to be taken back, and subjected to all the tortures of slavery. This in itself was enough to damp the ardor of my enthusiasm. But the loneliness overcame me. There I was in the midst of thousands, and yet a perfect stranger; without home and without friends, in the midst of thousands of my own brethren—children of a common Father, and yet I dared not to unfold to any one of them my sad condition. I was afraid to speak to any one for fear of speaking to the wrong one, and thereby falling into the hands of money-loving kidnappers, whose business it was to lie in wait for the panting fugitive, as the ferocious beasts of the forest lie in wait for their prey. The motto which I adopted when I started from slavery was this—"Trust no man!" I saw in every white man an enemy, and in almost every colored man cause for distrust. It was a most painful situation; and, to understand it, one must needs experience it, or imagine himself in similar circumstances. Let him be a fugitive slave in a strange land—a land given up to be the hunting-ground for slaveholders—whose inhabitants are legalized kidnappers—where he is every moment subjected to the terrible liability of being seized upon by his fellowmen, as the hideous crocodile seizes upon his prey!—I say, let him place himself in my situation—without home or friends—without money or credit—wanting shelter, and no one to give it—wanting bread, and no money to buy it,—and at the same time let him feel that he is pursued by merciless men-hunters, and in total darkness as to what to do, where to go, or where to stay,—perfectly helpless both as to the means of defence and means of escape,—in the midst of plenty, yet suffering the terrible gnawings of hunger,—in the midst of houses, yet having no home,—among fellow-men, yet feeling as if in the midst of wild beasts, whose greediness to swallow up the trembling and half-famished fugitive is only equalled by that with which the monsters of the deep swallow up the helpless fish upon which they subsist,—I say, let him be placed in this most trying situation,—the situation in which I was placed,—then, and not till then, will he fully appreciate the hardships of, and know how to sympathize with, the toil-worn and whip-scarred fugitive slave.

Thank Heaven, I remained but a short time in this distressed situation. I was relieved from it by the humane hand of MR. DAVID RUGGLES, whose vigilance, kindness, and perseverance, I shall never forget. I am glad of an opportunity to express, as far as words can, the love and gratitude I bear him. Mr. Ruggles is now afflicted with blindness, and is himself in need of the same kind offices which he was once so forward in the performance of toward others. I had been in New York but a few days, when Mr. Ruggles sought me out, and very kindly took me to his boarding-house at the corner of Church and Lespenard Streets. Mr. Ruggles was then very deeply engaged in the memorable *Darg* case, as well as attending to a number of other fugitive slaves, devising ways and means for their successful escape; and, though watched and hemmed in on almost every side, he seemed to be more than a match for his enemies.

Very soon after I went to Mr. Ruggles, he wished to know of me where I wanted to go; as he deemed it unsafe for me to remain in New York. I told him I was a calker, and should like to go where I could get work. I thought of going to Canada; but he decided against it, and in favor of my going to New Bedford, thinking I should be able to get work there at my trade. At this time, Anna,[1] my intended wife, came on; for I wrote to her immediately after my arrival at New York, (notwithstanding my homeless, houseless, and helpless condition,) informing her of my successful flight, and wishing her to come on forthwith. In a few days after her arrival, Mr. Ruggles called in the Rev. J. W. C. Pennington,

---

1. She was free.

who, in the presence of Mr. Ruggles, Mrs. Michaels, and two or three others, performed the marriage ceremony, and gave us a certificate, of which the following is an exact copy:—

"This may certify, that I joined together in holy matrimony Frederick Johnson[2] and Anna Murray, as man and wife, in the presence of Mr. David Ruggles and Mrs. Michaels.

JAMES W. C. PENNINGTON"
"*New York, Sept.* 15, 1838."

Upon receiving this certificate, and a five-dollar bill from Mr. Ruggles, I shouldered one part of our baggage, and Anna took up the other, and we set out forthwith to take passage on board of the steamboat John W. Richmond for Newport, on our way to New Bedford. Mr. Ruggles gave me a letter to a Mr. Shaw in Newport, and told me, in case my money did not serve me to New Bedford, to stop in Newport and obtain further assistance; but upon our arrival at Newport, we were so anxious to get to a place of safety, that, notwithstanding we lacked the necessary money to pay our fare, we decided to take seats in the stage, and promise to pay when we got to New Bedford. We were encouraged to do this by two excellent gentlemen, residents of New Bedford,

---

2. I had changed my name from Frederick *Bailey* to that of *Johnson*.

whose names I afterward ascertained to be Joseph Ricketson and William C. Taber. They seemed at once to understand our circumstances, and gave us such assurance of their friendliness as put us fully at ease in their presence. It was good indeed to meet with such friends, at such a time. Upon reaching New Bedford, we were directed to the house of Mr. Nathan Johnson, by whom we were kindly received, and hospitably provided for. Both Mr. and Mrs. Johnson took a deep and lively interest in our welfare. They proved themselves quite worthy of the name of abolitionists. When the stage-driver found us unable to pay our fare, he held on upon our baggage as security for the debt. I had but to mention the fact to Mr. Johnson, and he forthwith advanced the money.

We now began to feel a degree of safety, and to prepare ourselves for the duties and responsibilities of a life of freedom. On the morning after our arrival at New Bedford, while at the breakfast-table, the question arose as to what name I should be called by. The name give me by my mother was, "Frederick Augustus Washington Bailey." I, however, had dispensed with the two middle names long before I left Maryland so that I was generally known by the name of "Frederick Bailey." I started from Baltimore bearing the name of "Stanley." When

I got to New York, I again changed my name to "Frederick Johnson," and thought that would be the last change. But when I got to New Bedford, I found it necessary again to change my name. The reason of this necessity was, that there were so many Johnsons in New Bedford, it was already quite difficult to distinguish between them. I gave Mr. Johnson the privilege of choosing me a name, but told him he must not take from me the name of "Frederick." I must hold on to that, to preserve a sense of my identity. Mr. Johnson had just been reading the "Lady of the Lake," and at once suggested that my name be "Douglass." From that time until now I have been called "Frederick Douglass;" and as I am more widely known by that name than by either of the others, I shall continue to use it as my own.

I was quite disappointed at the general appearance of things in New Bedford. The impression which I had received respecting the character and condition of the people of the north, I found to be singularly erroneous. I had very strangely supposed, while in slavery, that few of the comforts, and scarcely any of the luxuries, of life were enjoyed at the north, compared with what were enjoyed by the slaveholders of the south. I probably came to this conclusion from the fact that northern people owned no slaves. I supposed that they were about upon a level with the non-slaveholding population of the south. I knew *they* were exceedingly poor, and I had been accustomed to regard their poverty as the necessary consequence of their being non-slaveholders. I had somehow imbibed the opinion that, in the absence of slaves, there could be no wealth, and very little refinement. And upon coming to the north, I expected to meet with a rough, hard-handed, and uncultivated population, living in the most Spartan-like simplicity, knowing nothing of the ease, luxury, pomp, and grandeur of southern slaveholders. Such being my conjectures, any one acquainted with the appearance of New Bedford may very readily infer how palpably I must have seen my mistake.

In the afternoon of the day when I reached New Bedford, I visited the wharves, to take a view of the shipping. Here I found myself surrounded with the strongest proofs of wealth. Lying at the wharves, and riding in the stream, I saw many ships of the finest model, in the best order, and of the largest size. Upon the right and left, I was walled in by granite warehouses of the widest dimensions, stowed to their utmost capacity with the necessaries and comforts of life. Added to this, almost every body seemed to be at work, but noiselessly so, compared with what I had been accustomed to in Baltimore. There were no loud songs heard from those engaged in loading and unloading ships. I heard no deep oaths or horrid curses on the laborer. I saw no whipping of men; but all seemed to go smoothly on. Every man appeared to understand his work, and went at it with a sober, yet cheerful earnestness, which betokened the deep interest which he felt in what he was doing, as well as a sense of his own dignity as a man. To me this looked exceedingly strange. From the wharves I strolled around and over the town, gazing with wonder and admiration at the splendid churches, beautiful dwellings, and finely-cultivated gardens; evincing an amount of wealth, comfort, taste, and refinement, such as I had never seen in any part of slaveholding Maryland.

Every thing looked clean, new, and beautiful. I saw few or no dilapidated houses, with poverty-stricken inmates; no half-naked children and bare-footed women, such as I had been accustomed to see in Hillsborough, Easton, St. Michael's, and Baltimore. The people looked more able, stronger, healthier, and happier, than those of Maryland. I was for once made glad by a view of extreme wealth, without being saddened by seeing extreme poverty. But the most astonishing as well as the most interesting thing to me was the condition of the colored people, a great many of whom, like myself, had escaped thither as a refuge from the hunters of men. I found many, who had not been seven years out of their chains, living in finer houses, and evidently enjoying more of the comforts of life, than the average of slaveholders in Maryland. I will venture to assert, that my friend Mr. Nathan Johnson (of whom I can say with a grateful heart, "I was hungry, and he gave me meat; I was thirsty, and he gave me drink; I was a stranger, and he took me in") lived in a neater house; dined at a better table; took, paid for, and read, more newspapers; better understood the moral, religious, and political character of the nation,—than nine tenths of the slaveholders in Talbot county Maryland. Yet Mr. Johnson was a working man. His hands were hardened by toil, and not his alone, but those also of Mrs. Johnson. I found the colored people much more spirited than I had supposed they would be. I found among them a determination to protect each other from the blood-thirsty kidnapper, at all hazards. Soon after my arrival, I was told of a circumstance which illustrated their spirit. A colored man and a fugitive slave were on unfriendly terms. The former was heard to threaten the latter with informing his master of his whereabouts. Straightway a meeting was called among the colored people, under the stereotyped notice, "Business of importance!" The betrayer was invited to attend.

The people came at the appointed hour, and organized the meeting by appointing a very religious old gentleman as president, who, I believe, made a prayer, after which he addressed the meeting as follows: *"Friends, we have got him here, and I would recommend that you young men just take him outside the door, and kill him!"* With this, a number of them bolted at him; but they were intercepted by some more timid than themselves, and the betrayer escaped their vengeance, and has not been seen in New Bedford since. I believe there have been no more such threats, and should there be hereafter, I doubt not that death would be the consequence.

I found employment, the third day after my arrival, in stowing a sloop with a load of oil. It was new, dirty, and hard work for me; but I went at it with a glad heart and a willing hand. I was now my own master. It was a happy moment, the rapture of which can be understood only by those who have been slaves. It was the first work, the reward of which was to be entirely my own. There was no Master Hugh standing ready, the moment I earned the money, to rob me of it. I worked that day with a pleasure I had never before experienced. I was at work for myself and newly-married wife. It was to me the starting-point of a new existence. When I got through with that job, I went in pursuit of a job of calking; but such was the strength of prejudice against color, among the white calkers, that they refused to work with me, and of course I could get no employment.[3] Finding my trade of no immediate benefit, I threw off my calking habiliments, and prepared myself to do any kind of work I could get to do. Mr. Johnson kindly let me have his wood-horse and saw, and I very soon found myself a plenty of work. There was no work too hard—none too dirty. I was ready to saw wood, shovel coal, carry the hod, sweep the chimney, or roll oil casks,—all of which I did for nearly three years in New Bedford, before I became known to the anti-slavery world.

In about four months after I went to New Bedford, there came a young man to me, and inquired if I did not wish to take the "Liberator." I told him I did; but, just having made my escape from slavery, I remarked that I was unable to pay for it then. I, however, finally became a subscriber to it. The paper came, and I read it from week to week with such feelings as it would be quite idle for me to attempt to describe. The paper became my meat and my drink. My soul was set all on fire. Its sympathy for my brethren in bonds—its scathing denunciations of slaveholders—its faithful exposures

---

3. I am told that colored persons can now get employment at calking in New Bedford—a result of anti-slavery effort.

of slavery—and its powerful attacks upon the upholders of the institution—sent a thrill of joy through my soul, such as I had never felt before!

I had not long been a reader of the "Liberator," before I got a pretty correct idea of the principles, measures and spirit of the anti-slavery reform. I took right hold of the cause. I could do but little; but what I could, I did with a joyful heart, and never felt happier than when in an anti-slavery meeting. I seldom had much to say at the meetings, because what I wanted to say was said so much better by others. But, while attending an anti-slavery convention at Nantucket, on the 11th of August, 1841, I felt strongly moved to speak, and was at the same time much urged to do so by Mr. William C. Coffin, a gentleman who had heard me speak in the colored people's meeting at New Bedford. It was a severe cross, and I took it up reluctantly. The truth was, I felt myself a slave, and the idea of speaking to white people weighed me down. I spoke but a few moments, when I felt a degree of freedom, and said what I desired with considerable ease. From that time until now, I have been engaged in pleading the cause of my brethren—with what success, and with what devotion, I leave those acquainted with my labors to decide.

APPENDIX

I find, since reading over the foregoing Narrative, that I have, in several instances, spoken in such a tone and manner, respecting religion, as may possibly lead those unacquainted with my religious views to suppose me an opponent of all religion. To remove the liability of such misapprehension, I deem it proper to append the following brief explanation. What I have said respecting and against religion, I mean strictly to apply to the *slave-holding religion* of this land, and with no possible reference to Christianity proper; for, between the Christianity of this land, and the Christianity of Christ, I recognize the widest possible difference— so wide, that to receive the one as good, pure, and holy, is of necessity to reject the other as bad, corrupt, and wicked. To be the friend of the one, is of necessity to be the enemy of the other. I love the pure, peaceable, and impartial Christianity of Christ: I therefore hate the corrupt, slaveholding, women-whipping, cradle-plundering, partial and hypocritical Christianity of this land. Indeed, I can see no reason, but the most deceitful one, for calling the religion of this land Christianity. I look upon it as the climax of all misnomers, the boldest of all frauds, and the grossest of all libels. Never was there a clearer case of "stealing the livery of the court of heaven to serve the devil in." I am filled with unutterable loathing when I contemplate the religious pomp and show, together with the horrible inconsistencies, which every where surround me. We have men-stealers for ministers, women-whippers for missionaries, and cradle-plunderers for church members. The man who wields the blood-clotted cowskin during the week fills the pulpit on Sunday, and claims to be a minister of the meek and lowly Jesus. The man who robs me of my earnings at the end of each week meets me as a class-leader on Sunday morning, to show me the way of life, and the path of salvation. He who sells my sister, for purposes of prostitution, stands forth as the pious advocate of purity. He who proclaims it a religious duty to read the Bible denies me the right of learning to read the name of the God who made me. He who is the religious advocate of marriage robs whole millions of its sacred influence, and leaves them to the ravages of wholesale pollution. The warm defender of the sacredness of the family relation is the same that scatters whole families,—sundering husbands and wives, parents and children, sisters and brothers,—leaving the hut vacant, and the hearth desolate. We see the thief preaching against theft, and the adulterer against adultery. We have men sold to build churches, women sold to support the gospel, and babes sold to purchase Bibles for the *poor heathen! all for the glory of God and the good of souls!* The slave auctioneer's bell and the church-going bell chime in with each other, and the bitter cries of the heart-broken slave are drowned in the religious shouts of his pious master. Revivals of religion and revivals in the slave-trade go hand in hand together. The slave prison and the church stand near each other. The clanking of fetters and the rattling of chains in the prison, and the pious psalm and solemn prayer in the church, may be heard at the same time. The dealers in the bodies and souls of men erect their stand in the presence of the pulpit, and they mutually help each other. The dealer gives his blood-stained gold to support the pulpit, and the pulpit, in return, covers his infernal business with the garb of Christianity.

Here we have religion and robbery the allies of each other—devils dressed in angels' robes, and hell presenting the semblance of paradise.

"Just God! and these are they,
  Who minister at thine altar, God of right!
Men who their hands, with prayer and blessing, lay
  On Israel's ark of light.

"What! preach, and kidnap men?
  Give thanks, and rob thy own afflicted poor?
Talk of thy glorious liberty, and then
  Bolt hard the captive's door?

"What! servants of thy own
  Merciful Son, who came to seek and save
The homeless and the outcast, fettering down
  The tasked and plundered slave!

"Pilate and Herod friends!
  Chief priests and rulers, as of old, combine!
Just God and holy! is that church which lends
  Strength to the spoiler thine?"

The Christianity of America is a Christianity, of whose votaries it may be as truly said, as it was of the ancient scribes and Pharisees, "They bind heavy burdens, and grievous to be borne, and lay them on men's shoulders, but they themselves will not move them with one of their fingers. All their works they do for to be seen of men.—They love the uppermost rooms at feasts, and the chief seats in the synagogues, ... and to be called of men, Rabbi, Rabbi.—But woe unto you, scribes and Pharisees, hypocrites! for ye shut up the kingdom of heaven against men; for ye neither go in yourselves, neither suffer ye them that are entering to go in. Ye devour widows' houses, and for a pretence make long prayers; therefore ye shall receive the greater damnation. Ye compass sea and land to make one proselyte, and when he is made, ye make him twofold more the child of hell than yourselves.—Woe unto you, scribes and Pharisees, hypocrites! for ye pay tithe of mint, and anise, and cumin, and have omitted the weightier matters of the law, judgment, mercy, and faith; these ought ye to have done, and not to leave the other undone. Ye blind guides! which strain at a gnat, and swallow a camel. Woe unto you, scribes and Pharisees, hypocrites! for ye make clean the outside of the cup and of the platter; but within, they are full of extortion and excess.—Woe unto you, scribes and Pharisees, hypocrites! for ye are like unto whited sepulchres, which indeed appear beautiful outward, but are within full of dead men's bones, and of all uncleanness. Even so ye also outwardly appear righteous unto men, but within ye are full of hypocrisy and iniquity."

Dark and terrible as is this picture, I hold it to be strictly true of the overwhelming mass of professed Christians in America. They strain at a gnat, and swallow a camel. Could any thing be more true of our churches? They would be shocked at the proposition of fellow-shipping a *sheep*-stealer; and at the same time they hug to their communion a *man*-stealer, and brand me with being an infidel, if I find fault with them for it. They attend with Pharisaical strictness to the outward forms of religion, and at the same time neglect the weightier matters of the law, judgment, mercy, and faith. They are always ready to sacrifice, but seldom to show mercy. They are they who are represented as professing to love God whom they have not seen, whilst they hate their brother whom they have seen. They love the heathen on the other side of the globe. They can pray for him, pay money to have the Bible put into his hand, and missionaries to instruct him; while they despise and totally neglect the heathen at their own doors.

Such is, very briefly, my view of the religion of this land; and to avoid any misunderstanding, growing out of the use of general terms, I mean, by the religion of this land, that which is revealed in the words, deeds, and actions, of those bodies, north and south, calling themselves Christian churches, and yet in union with slaveholders. It is against religion, as presented by these bodies, that I have felt it my duty to testify.

I conclude these remarks by copying the following portrait of the religion of the south, (which is, by communion and fellowship, the religion of the north,) which I soberly affirm is "true to the life," and without caricature or the slightest exaggeration. It is said to have been drawn, several years before the present anti-slavery agitation began, by a northern Methodist preacher, who, while residing at the south, had an opportunity to see slaveholding morals, manners, and piety, with his own eyes. "Shall I not visit for these things? saith the Lord. Shall not my soul be avenged on such a nation as this?"

"A PARODY.

"Come, saints and sinners, hear me tell
How pious priests whip Jack and Nell,
And women buy and children sell,
And preach all sinners down to hell,
   And sing of heavenly union.

"They'll bleat and baa, dona like goats,
Gorge down black sheep, and strain at motes,
Array their backs in fine black coats,
Then seize their negroes by their throats,
   And choke, for heavenly union.

155

"They'll church you if you sip a dram,
And damn you if you steal a lamb;
Yet rob old Tony, Doll, and Sam,
Of human rights, and bread and ham;
  Kidnapper's heavenly union.

"They'll loudly talk of Christ's reward,
And bind his image with a cord,
And scold, and swing the lash abhorred,
And sell their brother in the Lord
  To handcuffed heavenly union.

"They'll read and sing a sacred song,
And make a prayer both loud and long,
And teach the right and do the wrong,
Hailing the brother, sister throng,
  With words of heavenly union.

"We wonder how such saints can sing,
Or praise the Lord upon the wing,
Who roar, and scold, and whip, and sting,
And to their slaves and mammon cling,
  In guilty conscience union.

"They'll raise tobacco, corn, and rye,
And drive, and thieve, and cheat, and lie,
And lay up treasures in the sky,
By making switch and cowskin fly,
  In hope of heavenly union.

"They'll crack old Tony on the skull,
And preach and roar like Bashan bull,
Or braying ass, of mischief full,
Then seize old Jacob by the wool,
  And pull for heavenly union.

"A roaring, ranting, sleek man-thief,
Who lived on mutton, veal, and beef,
Yet never would afford relief
To needy, sable sons of grief,
  Was big with heavenly union.

"'Love not the world,' the preacher said,
And winked his eye, and shook his head;
He seized on Tom, and Dick, and Ned,
Cut short their meat, and clothes, and bread,
  Yet still loved heavenly union.

"Another preacher whining spoke
Of One whose heart for sinners broke:
He tied old Nanny to an oak,
And drew the blood at every stroke,
  And prayed for heavenly union.

"Two others oped their iron jaws,
And waved their children-stealing paws;
There sat their children in gewgaws;
By stinting negroes' backs and maws,
  They kept up heavenly union.

"All good from Jack another takes,
And entertains their flirts and rakes,
Who dress as sleek as glossy snakes,
And cram their mouths with sweetened cakes;
  And this goes down for union."

Sincerely and earnestly hoping that this little book may do something toward throwing light on the American slave system, and hastening the glad day of deliverance to the millions of my brethren in bonds—faithfully relying upon the power of truth, love, and justice, for success in my humble efforts— and solemnly pledging myself anew to the sacred cause,—I subscribe myself,

FREDERICK DOUGLASS.
LYNN, *Mass., April* 28, 1845.

The End

CONNECTIONS

What Is Your Fourth of July to Me?

Frederick Douglass

Fellow Citizens: Pardon me, and allow me to ask, why am I called upon to speak here today? What have I or those I represent to do with your national independence? Are the great principles of political freedom and of natural justice, embodied in that Declaration of Independence, extended to us? And am I, therefore, called upon to bring our humble offering to the national altar and to confess the benefits and express devout gratitude for the blessings resulting from your independence to us?

What to the American slave is your Fourth of July? I answer, a day that reveals to him, more than all other days of the year, the gross injustice and cruelty to which he is the constant victim. To him your celebration is a sham; your boasted liberty an unholy license; your national greatness, swelling vanity; your sounds of rejoicing are empty and heartless; your denunciation of tyrants, brass-fronted impudence; your shouts of liberty and equality, hollow mockery; your prayers and hymns, your sermons and thanksgivings, with all your religious parade and solemnity, are to him mere bombast, fraud, deception, impiety, and hypocrisy— a thin veil to cover up crimes which would disgrace a nation of savages. There is not a nation of the earth guilty of practices more shocking and bloody than are the people of these United States at this very hour.

Go where you may, search where you will, roam through all the monarchies and despotisms of the Old World, travel through South America, search out every abuse, and when you have found the last, lay your facts by the side of the everyday practices of this nation, and you will say with me that, for revolting barbarity and shameless hypocrisy, America reigns without a rival. . . .

—*Oration delivered in Corinthian Hall,*
Rochester, New York, July 5, 1852

■ ■ ■

"Two Tickets for Mr. Johnson and Slave"

Doreen Rappaport

This a true account of the escape of a couple named Craft, whose names were changed in this fictionalized account of their ordeal.

Ellen looked up from her sewing, out the small window of the cabin at the fallen darkness. William had worked late into the night for over three weeks now. It seemed everyone in town wanted something built in time for Christmas. Ellen was working extra hard too. Mrs. Collins was having three dinner parties and wanted a new dress for each one. Ellen went back to her sewing, with one ear listening for William.

It was three years since they had met, two since they'd married. Ellen had known early on that William loved her and felt sure she loved him, but when he first proposed, she refused. "It's not that I don't love you, William—I do. But . . ." she had said.

"Then why not?" he had asked.

"Because we can't really pledge our love. It's not ours to say forever. We can't even marry without our masters agreeing."

Eventually Ellen agreed to marriage, but not to having children. "They won't belong to us," she argued. "They can be taken away at Dr. Collins' whim. It's too cruel to them . . . and to us."

Ellen and William lived in Macon, the largest town in the center of Georgia. They had different masters but were allowed to live together in a cabin in the woods, behind Ellen's master's mansion. The cabin was plain and simple, but it was theirs unless their masters changed their minds. Like other town slaves, William was allowed to hire himself out, providing he paid his master $220 a year. Whatever he earned above that, he kept. William was a good cabinetmaker, and over the last three years had earned about $150 over what his master expected. Ellen's nimble hands worked exclusively for Mrs. Collins, busily sewing party dresses for her. Theirs was a much better life than that of plantation slaves, but it wasn't freedom.

She heard William hurrying up the path, faster than usual. She put her sewing aside.

"Ellen." He spoke excitedly as he came through the door. "I got it." He sat down next to her on a wooden bench he had made from odds and ends of wood left over from various jobs. "Got a plan to escape."

Over the past two years William and Ellen had talked a lot about escaping, but couldn't figure out a plan that seemed possible. Macon was in the deep south. It was many hundreds of miles to freedom in the North—miles of forests to walk through, rivers to wade across, mountains to climb and bounty hunters to hide from.

William took her hands in his. "Christmas is in eight days. We ask Dr. Collins and Mr. Taylor for a three-day pass. Tell 'em we want to visit friends on the Smith plantation. Like we did last year. I sure they agree. We escape then."

"But how?"

"You gonna take me up North. Slave owners can take their slaves anywhere they want." He stroked her soft cheeks. Ellen's skin was as white as his was dark. Her mother was a slave, but her father was a white man. Her grandfather had been white too. "Finest belles in Macon want skin like yours. No one gonna think you colored."

"But white women don't go traveling with colored men servants."

"No one gonna know you a woman." He wrapped his arms around her waist. "You be dressed up like a gentleman—top hat and all. A sickly but wealthy invalid white man goin' to Philadelphia. Hopin' to find some cure up North for his many ailments. And of course traveling with his nigger." He raised his eyebrows, like his master did when he was dressing him down. "No self-respecting gentleman, well or sick, go travelin' without his nigger."

"But where will I get these fine clothes?"

"What we can't buy, you sew. If need be, you sew trousers and a shirt grand enough for the best hotel. I find you a pair of boots and polish 'em till you can see your poor, pitiful face in them." He laughed. "And pitiful it'll be. All wrapped up with a bandage."

"Like I'm suffering from a toothache?"

William nodded.

Ellen's mouth broke into a grin. "I'll pretend I'm deaf, too. Then I won't have to talk much."

"But when you talk," said William, "it be real fine. Mrs. Collins always boastin' that her girl Ellen talk as good as any white lady in town." He pulled her toward him and held her in his arms.

Ellen had been in the big house since she was eleven, listening to her mistress and her friends gossip away the day while she tied her corset, buttoned her shoes and fluffed out her petticoats. When Ellen grew older, she was taught to sew, and in between the pinning and the hemming she overheard the talk of the women. Her ears took in the cadences, the rises and falls, in their way of talking, and she spoke as they did.

"Do you think it'll work, William? Do you really think I could fool people?"

"With the help of the Lord, we can do it."

Ellen's master agreed without hesitation to give her three days' holiday over Christmas. William's master complied somewhat grudgingly.

Buying gentlemen's clothes was not as easy. Georgia had a law forbidding white men to trade with slaves without a master's consent. But William knew which merchants in town disobeyed the law and traded with anybody who had money.

He went to different parts of town, at different times of the day, and to different stores. He bought the linen shirt and morning coat from a storekeeper he'd heard would sell a slave anything at the right price. He tricked another proprietor into believing he was buying a bow tie for his master. He bought the boots and socks from a house servant down the road. He couldn't find trousers small enough, so Ellen made her own, sewing long into the night, after she finished sewing for Mrs. Collins.

The night before they left, William polished the boots until they looked almost new. He cut Ellen's long hair off square in the back. She had no regrets as she wrapped the long locks up in a cloth and buried them in their mattress ticking.

Next morning, before the sun rose, Ellen slipped on the black socks. They were thin from wear. She stepped into the pants that she had so carefully stitched. The waist fit snug as she had planned, but the pant legs were baggy. She had deliberately made them that way to emphasize the impression of a frail gentleman.

She ran her fingers over the fine linen shirt. How beautifully made it was. No visible stitching around the collar or cuffs. The pleated front lay perfectly flat. Its small, even stitches looked more like decoration than necessity. She wondered how much William had paid for it.

"William," she whispered, waving the thin black tie. No one in the big house could ever hear their conversation, but this morning she wasn't taking any chances.

Out of the corner of her eye she watched William's large, muscular hands clumsily fold and refold the bow tie until it lay straight. His master had been right to have him trained to be a carpenter and not a house servant. She sat down on the bed and pulled up the boots. William had thickened the soles and hammered small heels onto the boots to give her more height. She walked around the room. Her feet weren't used to being so constricted. The leather rubbed slightly through the thin socks at both ankles.

No time to fuss now, she thought, putting on the black morning coat. She'd altered the shoulders to fit her better and tapered the sides slightly too, but left the jacket, like the pants, somewhat baggier than normal.

"How do I look?" She tucked her short hair under the top hat.

"Not finished yet." William handed her two large packets of herbs and meal wrapped in cloth. Ellen pressed the poultices to her chin while William wrapped a long white cloth over them. He pulled the cloth more tightly as it neared the top of her head, and then pulled it down around the other side of her face and back to her chin. With a few wrappings her cheeks and chin were completely covered. The cloth felt tight, but she didn't dare loosen it. It would loosen up some of its own accord anyway. If it loosened too much, it would separate and reveal her beardless face.

The final touch was an arm sling. Ellen didn't want anyone questioning why she couldn't sign her name. She might talk like a white Southerner, but she had never learned to read and write. Georgia law forbade teaching

slaves to read. Ellen was determined that once she got up
North, she would learn. And then she would teach other
black people to read too.

"Well, how do I look?"

"Sickly . . . but genteel," William answered.

He opened the cabin door and they peeked out. It was
barely dawn. Everything was still. Ellen put on dark-green
spectacles and walked out into the fresh morning air. They
tiptoed up the dirt path, and where it met the road, they
went off in different directions to the railroad station.

"Two tickets to Savannah for William Johnson and
slave." Ellen lowered her voice as much as she could but
still feared the stationmaster would know she was a
woman. But he didn't even look up as he pushed the
train tickets and some change toward her.

William helped his invalid master cross the platform
and mount the steps to the first-class coach. Ellen handed
him his ticket without looking at him, and he went off to
find the car where slaves were allowed to sit.

"Can I help you, sir?"

Ellen showed her ticket to the conductor. He led
her to a window seat. She knew she should give him a
coin or two for helping her to her seat, but her hands
were trembling so she didn't dare take money out of her
pocket. She tried to distract herself by looking out the
window.

"Fine morning, isn't it, sir?" said the man seated next
to her.

It was Mr. Cray—Dr. Collins' friend. He'd known her
since childhood. She'd seen him only two days ago when
he'd come to the big house for dinner. *What's he doing
here? Maybe they know we're here, and they've sent him to
get us.*

"Fine morning, isn't it, sir?" Mr. Cray repeated.

If I talk at all, he'll know it's me, thought Ellen.

"Fine morning, isn't it, sir?" Cray said again.

The man opposite Ellen laughed. "I think he's deaf."

Ellen knew Mr. Cray wouldn't care if he was deaf or not. He hated to be ignored. Cray tapped her on the shoulder. She knew she couldn't ignore him. She turned and looked at him. There was no recognition on his face that he knew her. *Amazing how white folks can see us all the time and never see us,* thought Ellen.

Mr. Cray raised his voice and, almost shouting, repeated his greeting for the fourth time.

"Yes," she mumbled, then turned her face to the window.

"Great deprivation, being deaf," said the man opposite Ellen.

"Certainly is." Cray felt generous toward the young invalid now that he'd broken through his deafness. He lunged into conversation with the other man. Ellen closed her eyes, trying to block out his words, praying he wouldn't try to involve her in conversation again. Twenty minutes later, when he got off the train, relief washed over her.

No one bothered the young invalid on the rest of the ride to Savannah. When the sun was almost down, the train pulled into the station in Savannah. A horse-drawn omnibus took the passengers to a hotel so they could have tea and pass the hour until the ferry for Charleston left. Mr. Johnson didn't feel well enough to go inside the hotel with the other passengers, so his servant brought his tea out to the bus.

An hour later they were shuttled to the wharf. William took Ellen directly to her berth on the steamship. Then he went to the gentlemen's lounge to prepare the rheumatism medicine.

"Where's your master?" asked a young military officer.

"He turned in, sir." William hoped his voice didn't reveal how nervous he felt.

"What's wrong with him?"

"Not feeling well. Ain't been well for a long time."

"He did look like a sickly sort," said another passenger.

"What's in that pot?" the officer asked, as the smell of camphor filled the room.

"Opodeldoc, sir."

"What's it for?"

"Rheumatism. My master got a terrible case."

"From the way that concoction smells, I should call it opodevil," said another man, laughing at his own joke. "Get it out of here now, or I'll throw it overboard."

William took the warmed medicine to Ellen's berth. She didn't say much in the little time William was with her, but he knew she was scared. He was scared too. He wanted to stay the night, hold her in his arms, reassure her, and himself, that their plan would work. But slaves didn't sleep with their masters in first-class berths. He kissed her good night and reluctantly left the cabin to search for a place to spend the night, for there were no sleeping accommodations for slaves. Near the bow of the boat he spotted a pile of sacks. He plopped down and felt warm air rising from a funnel behind. He closed his eyes and hoped no one would bother him till morning.

The next morning Ellen knew she could no longer postpone eating with the passengers without arousing suspicion. She felt worried. What if she couldn't pitch her voice deep enough to pass for a man? William helped the invalid to a seat at the captain's table.

"How are you feeling this morning, sir?" asked the captain.

"Better, thank you," she muttered.

"Well, I guess that awful-smelling medicine that your boy heated up did some good," said the young officer who'd questioned William in the lounge.

Ellen nodded. William stood at her side and cut her chicken into bite-sized pieces.

"Eat up, sir, it'll do you good," said the captain.

They don't know I'm a woman. She felt some relief. She looked down at the chicken and rice on her plate. *Hands, don't tremble.* She picked up her fork and stuck it into a small piece of chicken. William went to stand along the dining-room wall, waiting for his master's next command.

"Your boy's quite attentive," said the captain.

The man seated opposite Ellen leaned forward on his elbows. "Now sir, if you'd like to sell that there nigger, I'll buy him." He speared a large piece of chicken with his fork. "Just name your price." He bit into the chicken like a hungry dog.

Ellen gauged her reply. "I couldn't sell him, sir. I can't get on too well without him."

"I'm a slave trader, and I tell you he'll do you no good if you take him across Mason's and Dixon's line." He shook the small uneaten piece of chicken on his fork at her. "He's a keen nigger. I can see from the cut of his eye that he's certain to run away. You had better sell him to me."

"I think not, sir. I have great confidence in his fidelity."

"Fidevil!" the slave trader shouted, banging his fist on the table. It hit the edge of his saucer, and his coffee spilled on the lap of the man next to him. The scalded man jumped up. The slave trader dismissed the accident with a "Sorry neighbor, but accidents will happen in the best of families."

A bell clanged.

"We're in Charleston," said the captain.

"Let's go up on deck," suggested the officer.

Ellen didn't want to go on the deck. She didn't want to be in such a public place, didn't want to be in public view. If their masters had guessed they were missing, someone might be out there looking for them.

"Master . . ." William was at her side. Without a word, he led her to the gentlemen's lounge. Only when the crowd on the wharf thinned, and most passengers had left the boat, did Mr. Johnson's faithful servant help him off the boat to hail a carriage.

"Where to, sir?" asked the driver.

"Best hotel in town, and hurry." The arrogance in Ellen's voice surprised her. The driver soon deposited them at the Charleston Hotel.

"Stand aside." The hotel manager rushed from behind the reception desk, pushing William out of the way and offered his arm to the sickly-looking man. He snapped his fingers, and a servant braced Ellen on her other side.

"Now, what can I do for you, sir?"

"I need a room. A quiet one."

"For how long?"

"One night."

"Barnabas, take the gentleman to Room Four. Daniel, help Barnabas." The man looked at Ellen's arm sling. "Sir, if you'll just tell me your name, I'll gladly register for you."

If only that man knew his fuss was over a nigger! William fought an urge to laugh as he followed Ellen and her two helpers down the hall.

"He sure do think you one fine Southern gentleman." William began laughing as soon as the servants left them. Ellen pressed her hand over his mouth to stifle his laugh.

He playfully wrested her hand off his mouth. "No one can hear me."

"Can't tell," she whispered back. She took off her glasses and rubbed her eyes. "I'm so tired."

William knew how tired she was. Playacting every minute. Listening to her voice, watching her hand gestures, thinking about her walk. Worrying she'd give herself away with one wrong move. But he couldn't let her rest now. He slid off her arm sling, then unwrapped the face bandage. "You have to go to dinner, or that man gonna be suspicious."

She sighed. "All right."

William took the poultices and ran down the hall to the reception desk. "My master need these heated up."

The man rang a bell, and a slave appeared. "Barnabas, go down to the kitchen and get these heated up right off. Then take them to Room Four." He turned to William. "You can go back. Barnabas'll bring them down."

In a few minutes Barnabas knocked at their door. William opened it just enough to be able to take the poultices but to prevent Barnabas from seeing in. He put them on the mantelpiece. When they cooled, Ellen pressed them on her face and William rewrapped the cloth around her face. She slipped on the arm sling and hobbled off to the dining room. William left her at the dining-room entrance as two servants rushed to greet her.

She gonna be eatin' some beautiful bird and I lucky if I get a few scraps, he thought, walking to the kitchen.

Ellen stood on the ticket line in the Charleston train station and looked around. William stood off to the side. The young military officer who had sat at her table on the steamer was two places behind her on the line talking to the steamer captain. The two men caught her glance and nodded. She returned the greeting, then turned away. The

line moved forward. In a few minutes she was at the ticket
window.

"Two tickets for Philadelphia, via Wilmington, for
Mr. Johnson and slave." Her supposed name rang false
in her ears.

The customs officer looked at her, then signaled William
to come over. "Boy, do you belong to this gentleman?"

"Yes, sir."

The customs officer handed the tickets to Ellen and
opened a large ledger. "Sir, I need you to sign your name
and the name of your boy in this here book. And I need
a dollar duty on your boy."

Ellen reached awkwardly into her pocket. "Here's my
dollar, but you must sign for me. I can't do much writing
with my hand wrapped like this."

"Can't do that, sir. Law wants your signature, not mine."

Her eyes darted nervously behind the dark glasses.

"Well, that's a silly law," bellowed the military officer,
coming forward from his place in line. "I'll vouch for
Mr. Johnson," he snapped at the customs officer as if
dressing down a disobedient soldier. "Know his kin like
a book, and I think, sir"—he pointed a finger at the
man—"that you know me and my kin, so there shouldn't
be any trouble here for my friend Mr. Johnson."

"I'll vouch for him too." The steamer captain was at her
side. "Be glad to register this gentleman's name and take
full responsibility." The captain took the book and signed
it. Then he turned to Ellen. "It's all right now, sir."

"Thank you kindly." Her words came slow and stilted.

"Hope you don't think that he intended any disrespect,
sir. We make it a rule to be very strict in Charleston. Got
to. Too many damned abolitionists around who want to
run off with our niggers." The captain offered his arm for
Mr. Johnson to lean on.

The overnight trip to Wilmington, North Carolina, was uneventful. The next morning, when they changed to a train for Richmond, Virginia, no one objected as the slave settled his frail master into an empty compartment that had a couch that was set aside for families and invalids.

Ellen stretched out across the seat. It was Christmas Eve. Tomorrow their passes expired. When they didn't return home, their owners would know they had escaped and would send the slave hunters after them. What if there were delays and they didn't reach Philadelphia in time?

At Petersburg, Virginia, her restless nap was disturbed by an older man and his two young daughters. "Please, sir, don't," said the darker-haired daughter as Ellen made room for her on the couch. "Stay there and rest yourself."

And avoid conversation, too, thought Ellen.

"Would you like my shawl for a pillow?" the girl offered.

"Take mine, too," offered the other daughter.

Good old Southern hospitality. Ellen lay back on the couch and pretended to sleep. Her eyes were closed, but she sensed the girls' eyes on her. After a while she got up.

"May I be so bold, sir, as to ask what ails you?" said the father.

"Inflammatory rheumatism, sir."

"I know it well." The man took out a pencil and paper and began writing.

"Where are you going, sir?" asked the dark-haired daughter. Ellen felt the girls' eyes trying to penetrate her dark glasses.

"Hush now, girls," the father reproached his daughters gently. "This gentleman's got a lot on his mind." He offered a paper to Ellen. "Sir, this recipe is the perfect cure for rheumatism. Always put it on when I feel a touch coming."

Ellen would have gladly faked reading the perfect cure to make the man happy, but since she couldn't read, she didn't know which way to hold the paper. She thanked him profusely and tucked it into her waistcoat pocket.

At Richmond the gentleman and his daughters got off the train, and a stout, elderly woman and a young man took their seats. No sooner was the woman seated than she sprang up and pulled down the window. "There goes my nigger, Ned! That no-good runaway!"

Poor Ned! Ellen looked out the window. Her heart sank. William was walking on the platform. The woman had mistaken him for her slave. "No, that's my boy," she said nervously.

"Ned, you come back here, you rascal!" the woman shouted at William.

"Madam, that's *my* boy, William, not your Ned!"

The woman drew her head in. "I beg your pardon, sir. I was so sure it was my nigger. Never in my life saw two black pigs more alike than your boy and my Ned."

The train pulled away from the station. The woman leaned back in the seat and closed her eyes. "Sir, I hope your boy won't turn out to be as worthless as my Ned. I was as kind to him as if he had been my own son. It grieves me to think that after all I did for him, he ran off."

"When did he leave you?" asked the man.

"About eighteen months ago. A few months after I sold his wife." She sighed. "She was as good and faithful a nigger as you could wish for. And beautiful too. . . . Whiter than I am. Whiter than both of you."

"Then why did you sell her?" asked the man.

"Had to. The poor thing got so ill she couldn't work."

The man waited a minute before he spoke again. "Since she was *so* faithful, and served you *so* well, why didn't you free her so she could live out her sickly life in a bit of ease?"

"Freeing niggers is the worst thing you can do for them. Just before my dear husband died, he decided to free ours. I knew he wasn't in his right mind to do that, so I had the will changed back." She pursed her lips and shook her head back and forth, like Mrs. Collins did when she was getting ready to complain about something. "Niggers are more trouble than they're worth. Ten of mine have run away since my poor husband died."

Lord keep them free, thought Ellen.

"My son, poor boy, he lives up north now, in New York. He says that my slaves are much better off than the free ones there."

"Then I have no doubt that your Ned and the other nine will realize their mistake and return home." Ellen felt that the man was holding back laughing.

An hour later, when the woman left the train, the man turned to Ellen. "Damn shame. That old bag cheating those poor Negroes out of their liberty."

Ellen liked him but refrained from further conversation.

At Washington, D.C., William and Ellen took the train for Baltimore, Maryland. When they arrived, William went to check that their luggage would follow them to Philadelphia.

"Where you going, boy?" A military officer blocked his way.

William sprang to attention. "Philadelphia, sir."

"What are you going there for?"

"Goin' with my master, sir."

"Bring him to me, boy. And be quick about it. Your train's ready to leave."

William ran to get Ellen who was seated in the crowded waiting room. "Master, a gentleman would like to see you." His voice was calm, but fear showed in his eyes. She leaned on him to get up, and he led her to the officer.

"My boy told me you wanted to see me." Ellen was afraid, but they were so close to freedom she wasn't going to let this bully ruin everything.

"Yes, sir. It's against our rules, sir, to allow anyone to take a slave out of Baltimore into Philadelphia unless we're satisfied that he has a right to do so."

"Why is that?"

"Because if the gentleman traveling with the slave turns out *not* to be his rightful owner, and if the rightful owner comes here and proves that his slave got through here, law says we have to pay him for the slave."

"Isn't it obvious that I am a slaveholder?" she said indignantly.

"Of course it's obvious," said an interested passenger.

"Let him go," said another passenger. "Can't you see he's an invalid?"

"I bought my tickets in Charleston," Ellen continued in the same angry tone. "They questioned me there at length. You have no right to do so now."

"Well, sir, right or wrong, I'm doing it."

"This is ridiculous . . . and insulting." She summoned up the arrogance she had heard all her life.

"Do you know anyone in Baltimore who could vouch for you?"

"Ask that man over there." She pointed haughtily to the conductor of the train they had been on.

The man hurried over to the conductor. The bell rang for the train. *Please, dear Lord.*

The officer hurried back. "I guess it's all right for you to go. Your being so ill and all. And the conductor remembers you well."

"I would hope so." Ellen hobbled across the platform as quickly as possible. William helped her into one of the first-class carriages, then ran along the platform looking for the car for free coloreds and slaves. There was none. He ended up in the luggage car. Tiredness caught up with him, and he fell asleep.

Ellen drifted off for a few hours, but when she awakened, it was dark and cold. She felt scared. She rang for the conductor. "Can you find my boy?"

"Haven't seen him for some time."

"Find him for me," she ordered.

"I'm no slave hunter."

"Call the porter," she said firmly.

The porter found William in the luggage car. "Wake up. Your master's looking for you." He laughed. "That white man sure is scared." He lowered his voice to a whisper. "Brother, we're pulling into Philadelphia. I'll tell him I didn't find you, and I'll hide you till he leaves the station."

"Can't do that to my master. He need me more than anyone."

"Are you mad? One nigger's the same to a white man as another." William didn't respond. The porter shook his head in disbelief. "Well, if you change your mind, go to Thirty-one North Fifth Street. They'll be real friendly to you."

"I remember that. Thank you, brother."

The bell clanged as they pulled into the station. William hurried through the cars to find Ellen. No one paid attention as the husky black man helped his invalid master off the train. No one heard him hail a carriage and confidently tell the driver, "Thirty-one North Fifth Street, please."

Abolitionist William Lloyd Garrison wrote up the Crafts' daring escape in his newspaper The Liberator, *and the Crafts began telling their story in cities and towns across the United States. In 1850, fearing that they could be captured and returned to their masters under the provisions of the soon-to-be passed Fugitive Slave Act, they moved to England. After the Civil War they returned to the United States, bought a former Georgia plantation and set up a school for black children and adults.*

▪ ▪ ▪

Incident
Countee Cullen

Once riding in old Baltimore,
    Heart-filled, head-filled with glee,
I saw a Baltimorean
    Keep looking straight at me.

Now I was eight and very small,
    And he was no whit bigger,
And so I smiled, but he poked out
    His tongue, and called me, "Nigger."

I saw the whole of Baltimore
    From May until December;
Of all the things that happened there
    That's all that I remember.

■ ■ ■

Learning the Game

Francisco Jiménez

I was in a bad mood. It was the last day of seventh grade before summer vacation. I had known the day was coming, but I had tried not to think about it because it made me sad. For my classmates, it was a happy day. During the afternoon, Miss Logan asked for volunteers to share what they were going to do during the summer; lots of hands went up. Some talked about going away on trips; others about summer camp. I folded my hands under the desk, lowered my head, and tried not to listen. After a while, I managed to tune out what they were saying and only heard faint voices coming from different parts of the room.

In the school bus on the way home, I took out my note pad and pencil from my shirt pocket and began figuring out how much time before I would start school again— from the middle of June until the first week of November, about four and a half months. Ten weeks picking strawberries in Santa Maria and another eight weeks harvesting grapes and cotton in Fresno. As I added the number of days, I started to get a headache. Looking out the window I said to myself, "One-hundred-thirty-two more days after tomorrow."

As soon as I arrived home, I took two of Papá's aspirins and lay down. I had just closed my eyes when I heard Carlos, our neighbor, shouting outside. "Come on, Panchito, we're starting the game."

The game was kick-the-can. I played it with Carlos and my younger brothers, Trampita, Torito, and Rubén, on school days when I had no homework, and on weekends when I was not too tired from working in the fields.

"Hurry, or else!" Carlos hollered impatiently.

I liked the game, but I did not enjoy playing with Carlos. He was older than I, and often reminded me of it, especially when I disagreed with him. If we wanted to play, we had to follow his rules. No one could play unless he said so. He wore tight jeans and a white t-shirt with the sleeves rolled up to show off his muscles. Under his right sleeve, he tucked a cigarette pack.

"Come on Panchito!" Trampita yelled. "You're making us wait."

I went outside to play. I wanted to forget about the next 133 days.

"It's about time," Carlos said, giving me a light punch on the right shoulder. "You'll be the guard," he said, pointing at Rubén. "Trampita, you draw the circle. Torito, you get the can." As Carlos was giving orders, I saw Manuelito standing by one of the garbage cans. During every game, he stood by himself on the sidelines because Carlos would not let him play. "Let Manuelito be the guard," I said to Carlos.

"No way," he responded annoyingly. "I already told you before, he can't play. He's too slow."

"Come on, Carlos, let him play," I insisted.

"No!" he shouted, giving me and Manuelito a dirty look.

"Go ahead and play, Panchito," Manuelito said timidly. "I'll stand here and watch."

We started the game, and the more we played, the less I thought about my troubles. Even my headache went away. We played until dark.

The alarm clock went off early the next morning. I glanced at the window. It was still dark outside. I shut my eyes, trying to get one more minute of sleep, but Roberto, my older brother, jumped out of bed and pulled off the covers. "Time to get up!" he said. When I saw him putting on his work clothes, I remembered we were going to work, and not to school. My shoulders felt heavy.

On the way to the fields, Papá turned on the *Carcachita's* headlights to see through the thick fog that blew in from the coast. It covered the valley every morning, like a large, gray sheet. Ito, the sharecropper, was waiting for us when we arrived. Then a black pickup truck appeared. We could see it through the wall of fog, not far from where we parked. The driver stopped behind our *Carcachita* and, in perfect Spanish, ordered the passenger who rode in the bed of the truck to get off.

"Who's that?" I asked Papá, pointing to the driver.

"Don't point," Papá said. "It's bad manners. He's Mr. Díaz, the *contratista*. He runs the *bracero* camp for Sheehey Berry Farms. The man with him is one of the *braceros*."

In his broken Spanish, Ito introduced us to Gabriel, the man who accompanied the *contratista*.

Gabriel looked a few years older than Roberto. He wore a pair of loose, tan pants and a blue shirt. The shirt was faded. His straw hat was slightly tilted to the right and he had long, dark sideburns that were trimmed and came down to the middle of his square jaw. His face was weather-beaten. The deep cracks in the back of his heels were as black as the soles of his *huaraches*.

Gabriel took off his hat and we shook hands. He seemed nervous. But he relaxed when we greeted him in Spanish.

After the *contratista* left, we marched in line to the end of the field, selected a row, and started to work. Gabriel ended up between Papá and me. Because it was Gabriel's first time harvesting strawberries, Ito asked Papá to show him how to pick. "It's easy, Don Gabriel," Papá said. "The main thing is to make sure the strawberry is ripe and not bruised or rotten. And when you get tired from squatting, you can pick on your knees." Gabriel learned quickly by watching and following Papá.

At noon, Papá invited Gabriel to join us for lunch in our *Carcachita*. He sat next to me in the back seat while Roberto and Papá sat in the front. From his brown paper bag, he pulled out a Coke and three sandwiches: one of mayonnaise and two of jelly. "Not again! We get this same lunch from that Díaz every day," he complained. "I am really tired of this."

"You can have one of my *taquitos*," I said.

"Only if you take this jelly sandwich," he responded, handing it to me. I looked at Papá's face. When I saw him smile, I took it and thanked him.

"Do you have a family, Don Gabriel?" Papá asked.

"Yes, and I miss them a lot," he answered. "Especially my three kids."

"How old are they?" Papá asked.

"The oldest is five, the middle one is three, and the little one, a girl, is two."

"And you, Don Pancho, how many do you have?"

"A handful," Papá answered, grinning. "Five boys and a girl. All living at home."

"You're lucky. You get to see them every day," Gabriel said. "I haven't seen mine for months." He continued as though thinking out loud. "I didn't want to leave them, but I had no choice. We have to eat, you know. I send them a few dollars every month for food and things. I'd like to send them more, but after I pay Díaz for room and board and transportation, little is left." Then in an angry tone of voice he added, "Díaz is a crook. He over charges for everything. That *sin vergüenza*[1] doesn't know who he's dealing with."

At this point, we heard the honking of a car horn. It was Ito signaling us that it was time to go back to work. Our half-hour lunch break was over.

That evening, and for several days after, I was too tired to play outside when we got home from work. I went straight to bed after supper. But as I got more and more

---

1. **sin vergüenza** (Spanish): shameless person

▪▪

used to picking strawberries, I began to play kick-the-can
again. The game was always the same. We played by
Carlos's rules and he refused to let Manuelito play.

Work was always the same, too. We picked from
six o'clock in the morning until six in the afternoon. Even
though the days were long, I looked forward to seeing
Gabriel and having lunch with him every day. I enjoyed
listening to him tell stories and talk about Mexico. He was
as proud of being from the state of Morelos as my father
was about being from Jalisco.

One Sunday, near the end of the strawberry season, Ito
sent me to work for a sharecropper who was sick and needed
extra help that day. His field was next to Ito's. Gabriel was
loaned out to the same farmer. As soon as I arrived, the
contratista began giving me orders. "Listen, *hüerquito*, I
want you to hoe weeds. But first, give me and Gabriel a
hand," he said. Gabriel and I climbed on to the bed of the
truck and helped him unload a plow. The *contratista* tied
one end of a thick rope to it and, handing the other end to
Gabriel, said, "Here, tie this around your waist. I want you
to till the furrows."

"I can't do that," Gabriel said with a painful look in
his face.

"What do you mean you can't?" responded the
contratista, placing his hands on his hips.

"In my country, oxen pull plows, not men," Gabriel
replied, tilting his hat back. "I am not an animal."

The *contratista* walked up to Gabriel and yelled in his
face, "Well this isn't your country, idiot! You either do what I
say or I'll have you fired!"

"Don't do that, please," Gabriel said. "I have a family
to feed."

"I don't give a damn about your family!" the *contratista*
replied, grabbing Gabriel by the shirt collar and pushing

him. Gabriel lost his balance and fell backwards. As he hit the ground, the *contratista* kicked him in the side with the tip of his boot. Gabriel sprung up and, with both hands clenched, lunged at the *contratista*. White as a ghost, Díaz quickly jumped back. "Don't be stupid . . . your family," he stammered. Gabriel held back. His face was flushed with rage. Without taking his eyes off Gabriel, the *contratista* slid into his truck and sped off, leaving us in a cloud of dust.

I felt scared. I had not seen men fight before. My mouth felt dry and my hands and legs began to shake. Gabriel threw his hat on the ground and said angrily, "That Díaz is a coward. He thinks he's a big man because he runs the *bracero* camp for the growers. He's nothing but a leech! And now he tries to treat me like an animal. I've had it." Then, picking up his hat and putting it on, he added, "He can cheat me out of my money. He can fire me. But he can't force me to do what isn't right. He can't take away my dignity. That he can't do!"

All day, while Gabriel and I hoed weeds, I kept thinking about what happened that morning. It made me angry and sad. Gabriel cursed as he hacked at the weeds.

When I got home from work that evening, I felt restless. I went outside to play kick-the-can. "Come on guys, let's play!" Carlos yelled out, resting his right foot on the can.

I went up to Manuelito who was sitting on the ground and leaning against one of the garbage cans. "You heard Carlos, let's play," I said loudly so that Carlos could hear me.

"He didn't mean me," Manuelito answered, slowly getting up.

"Yes, you too," I insisted.

"Is it true, Carlos?" Manuelito asked.

"No way!" Carlos shouted.

Manuelito put his hands in his pockets and walked away.

"If Manuelito doesn't play, I won't either," I said. As soon as I said it, my heart started pounding. My knees felt weak. Carlos came right up to me. He had fire in his eyes. "Manuelito doesn't play!" he yelled.

He stuck his right foot behind my feet and pushed me. I fell flat on my back. My brothers rushed over to help me up. "You can push me around, but you can't force me to play!" I yelled back, dusting off my clothes and walking away. Trampita, Torito, Rubén, and Manuelito followed me to the front of our barrack.

Carlos stood alone inside the circle in the dirt, looking at the can and glancing at us once in a while. After a few moments, he cocked his head back, spat on the ground, and swaggered toward us saying, "OK, Manuelito can play."

Screaming with joy, Manuelito and my brothers jumped up and down like grasshoppers. I felt like celebrating, too, but I held back. I did not want Carlos to see how happy I was.

The following morning, when Ito told us that the *contratista* had gotten Gabriel fired and sent back to Mexico, I felt like someone had kicked me in the stomach. I could not concentrate on work. At times I found myself not moving at all. By the time I had picked one crate, Papá had picked two. He finished his row, started a second, and caught up to me.

"What's the matter, Panchito?" he asked. "You're moving too slow. You need to speed it up."

"I keep thinking about Gabriel," I answered.

"What Díaz did was wrong, and someday he'll pay for it, if not in this life, in the next one," he said. "Gabriel did what he had to do."

Papá pushed me along, handing me several handfuls of strawberries he picked from my row. With his help, I got through that long day.

When we got home from work, I did not want to play kick-the-can. I wanted to be alone, but my brothers would not let me. They followed me around, asking me to play.

I finally gave in when Manuelito came over and joined them. "Please, just one game," he pleaded.

"OK, just one," I answered.

We drew sticks to see who would play guard. Carlos was it. When he counted to twenty with his eyes closed, we ran and hid. I went behind a pepper tree that was next to the outhouse. When Carlos spotted me, he shouted, "I spy Panchito!" We both raced to the can. I got to it first and kicked it with all my might. It went up in the air and landed in one of the garbage cans. That was the last time I played the game.

■ ■ ■

Trapped in a Hellhole
Stan Grossfeld

The brass factories are all unmarked, down alleyways framed by streams of urine baking under windows covered by bars. This is the 19th century revisited. Furnaces belch molten lava and acrid smoke attacks the eyes and throat. On the edge of the darkness, a 10-year-old boy, his brown body turned black with soot, is making a brass angel while living in hell. For this, he is at least paid a pittance every week, 30 rupees, or about a dollar. But for the 10 million children who toil throughout India as virtual slaves, there is no compensation.

"I was kidnapped," says eight-year-old Laxmi Sada at Mukti Ashram, a home for freed slaves. "Me and three more boys were playing outside the village and some people came and gave us something to eat and said they had even better things to eat. They took us in a bus. I didn't even know what a carpet factory was. I started crying. Many times I was beaten. It was the master who first hit me with the punja (a comb-like tool), and the blood came down . . . then they would put matchstick powder on the wound and light it to stop the bleeding. I never saw the sun rise." Sometimes Laxmi went to the bathroom in his pants. "If you got up, you'd get beaten." Laxmi's father came to the factory to rescue him, but factory goons intercepted him. "I saw my father being beaten. He could not recover. My father wanted to take me and put me on his lap. Why did he have to die? I was there one year. Now I say, long live the revolution, stop child slavery. I want to kill the master. Because of him I couldn't see my father."

Some 50,000 children toil six days a week for a few dollars a month in factories throughout Moradabad, four hours east of New Delhi. The children choke on noxious fumes that carry tuberculosis and other respiratory diseases.

"Nobody lives to be 40," says Karan Singh, a human rights worker. Behind these doors, children make miniature Statues of Liberty, and busts of John F. Kennedy. The irony is that India—the world's largest democracy—is doing virtually nothing to enforce a 1986 law that prohibits children younger than 14 from working.

"It's very frustrating," said Kailash Satyarthi, chairman of the South Asian Coalition on Child Servitude, an umbrella organization responsible for the rescue of 26,000 children. "The law is there but the government doesn't want to implement it. Sometimes the fine is less than $2. So you're using a child's life for a $2 fine."

"They say the parents need the children to work to get by, but that's not true because there are 50,000 children working here while 50,000 adults are unemployed. We need to give those jobs to the adults and let the kids go to school," says Ashutosh Chakrapani, a coalition worker. The International Labor Organization estimates there are some 200 million child laborers under the age of 15 worldwide. Many of these are bonded laborers, that is, unpaid slaves. They don't get paid wages, they don't get paid on a piece-work scale. They are lured away from their parents, who are told they are going to go to school to be trained for a job. The parents are given a small loan with high interest that they can't repay. Sometimes they are given nothing. Udai Ram, 9, of Bihar says, "A middleman came to my village and told my father I would be taken to school to learn things. They promised him a 50-rupee advance. He never got it.

"When I went in there the first time there was a thick cloud. I saw this beautiful carpet and I wanted to sit on it and I was beaten. I worked till 12 midnight. The master was teaching and I made many mistakes. The master would hit my finger with a very sharp knife. Once he cut the small tip off."

Udai said he worked with 11 other boys in a factory with three looms. "I always wanted to cry. I'd think about a beautiful forest and a river with my friends making balls of sand.

"My master is free. While I was working, I saw he got a new car and a new truck. It was like being in a cage. Have you seen birds fly? Now I'm out of the cage. I have never seen an adult make a carpet.". . .

"Nimble fingers have nothing to do with the knotting," says Satyarthi, rebutting the claim that child weavers make smaller knots and thus produce higher quality rugs. The more knots in the less space, the finer the carpet. Tighter knots are made by strong men." . . . [I]mporters and retailers say it is impossible to certify that the carpets are made without child labor. . . .

"If people keep buying carpets, they are guilty of perpetrating child slavery," says Satyarthi. "We're telling people that with these shining carpets, most of the shining comes from the blood of the children."

from "Trapped in a Hellhole", The Boston Globe,
December 29, 1994

■ ■ ■

Women

Alice Walker

They were women then
My mama's generation
Husky of voice—Stout of
Step
With fists as well as
Hands
How they battered down
Doors
And ironed
Starched white
Shirts
How they led
Armies
Headragged Generals
Across mined
Fields
Booby-trapped
Ditches
To discover books
Desks
A place for us
How they knew what we
Must know
Without knowing a page
Of it
Themselves.

■ ■ ■

Letter from a Freedman
to His Old Master

(Written just as he dictated it.)

Jourdon Anderson

Dayton, Ohio, August 7, 1865.

To my old Master, Colonel P. H. Anderson, *Big Spring,*
Tennessee.

Sir: I got your letter, and was glad to find that you had not
forgotten Jourdon, and that you wanted me to come back
and live with you again, promising to do better for me than
anybody else can. I have often felt uneasy about you. I
thought the Yankees would have hung you long before this,
for harboring Rebs they found at your house. I suppose they
never heard about your going to Colonel Martin's to kill the
Union soldier that was left by his company in their stable.
Although you shot at me twice before I left you, I did not
want to hear of your being hurt, and am glad you are still
living. It would do me good to go back to the dear old home
again, and see Miss Mary and Miss Martha and Allen, Esther,
Green, and Lee. Give my love to them all, and tell them I
hope we will meet in the better world, if not in this. I would
have gone back to see you all when I was working in the
Nashville Hospital, but one of the neighbours told me that
Henry intended to shoot me if he ever got a chance.

I want to know particularly what the good chance is
you propose to give me. I am doing tolerably well here. I
get twenty-five dollars a month, with victuals and clothing;
have a comfortable home for Mandy,—the folks call her
Mrs. Anderson,—and the children—Milly, Jane, and
Grundy—go to school and are learning well. The teacher
says Grundy has a head for a preacher. They go to Sunday
school, and Mandy and me attend church regularly. We are

kindly treated. Sometimes we overhear others saying, "Them colored people were slaves" down in Tennessee. The children feel hurt when they hear such remarks; but I tell them it was no disgrace in Tennessee to belong to Colonel Anderson. Many darkeys would have been proud, as I used to be, to call you master. Now if you will write and say what wages you will give me, I will be better able to decide whether it would be to my advantage to move back again.

As to my freedom, which you say I can have, there is nothing to be gained on that score, as I got my free papers in 1864 from the Provost-Marshal-General of the Department of Nashville. Mandy says she would be afraid to go back without some proof that you were disposed to treat us justly and kindly; and we have concluded to test your sincerity by asking you to send us our wages for the time we served you. This will make us forget and forgive old scores, and rely on your justice and friendship in the future. I served you faithfully for thirty-two years, and Mandy twenty years. At twenty-five dollars a month for me, and two dollars a week for Mandy, our earnings would amount to eleven thousand six hundred and eighty dollars. Add to this the interest for the time our wages have been kept back, and deduct what you paid for our clothing, and three doctor's visits to me, and pulling a tooth for Mandy, and the balance will show what we are in justice entitled to. Please send the money by Adam's Express, in care of V. Winters, Esq., Dayton, Ohio. If you fail to pay us for faithful labors in the past, we can have little faith in your promises in the future. We trust the good Maker has opened your eyes to the wrongs which you and your fathers have done to me and my fathers, in making us toil for you for generations without recompense. Here I draw my wages every Saturday night; but in Tennessee there was never any pay-day for the negroes any more than for the horses and cows. Surely there will be a day of reckoning for those who defraud the laborer of his hire.

In answering this letter, please state if there would be any safety for my Milly and Jane, who are now grown up, and both good-looking girls. You know how it was with poor Matilda and Catherine. I would rather stay here and starve—and die, if it come to that—than have my girls brought to shame by the violence and wickedness of their young masters. You will also please state if there has been any schools opened for the colored children in your neighborhood. The great desire of my life now is to give my children an education, and have them form virtuous habits.

Say howdy to George Carter, and thank him for taking the pistol from you when you were shooting at me.

From your old servant,
Jourdon Anderson

■ ■ ■

Learning to Read
Frances E. W. Harper

Very soon the Yankee teachers
    Came down and set up school;
But, oh! how the Rebs did hate it,—
    It was agin' their rule.

Our masters always tried to hide
    Book learning from our eyes;
Knowledge did'nt agree with slavery—
    'Twould make us all too wise.

But some of us would try to steal
    A little from the book,
And put the words together,
    And learn by hook or crook.

I remember Uncle Caldwell,
    Who took pot-liquor fat
And greased the pages of his book,
    And hid it in his hat.

And had his master ever seen
    The leaves upon his head,
He'd have thought them greasy papers,
    But nothing to be read.

And there was Mr. Turner's Ben,
    Who heard the children spell,
And picked the words right up by heart,
    And learned to read 'em well.

Well, the Northern folks kept sending
        The Yankee teachers down;
And they stood right up and helped us,
        Though Rebs did sneer and frown.

And, I longed to read my Bible,
        For precious words it said;
But when I begun to learn it,
        Folks just shook their heads,

And said there is no use trying,
        Oh! Chloe, you're too late;
But as I was rising sixty,
        I had no time to wait.

So I got a pair of glasses,
        And straight to work I went,
And never stopped till I could read
        The hymns and Testament.

Then I got a little cabin—
        A place to call my own—
And I felt as independent
        As the queen upon her throne.

■ ■ ■

Frederick Douglass

(1818–1895)

Despite being born into slavery, Frederick Douglass (born
Frederick Augustus Washington Bailey) gained freedom
and an education and inspired others through his oratory
and his life. Douglass fought hard for his freedom, as did
many others like him, but what makes Douglass such an
extraordinary figure in history is the fact that his struggle
was to become an inspiration for all who believe in
equality for all peoples.

Douglass was a young man of nineteen when he escaped from slavery and began to build a new life as a free
man. Eager to help other slaves, he attended abolitionist
meetings and read their newspapers. Three years after his
escape, at one such meeting, Douglass was asked to speak
about his experiences. That meeting and Douglass's speech
changed the young man's life forever. Douglass began a
career as a speaker for the abolitionist movement, traveling widely to denounce slavery. He not only criticized
slavery; he shared his personal experiences and private
emotions and became renowned for his oratory, moving
entire audiences to tears with his words.

A great believer in the power of the written word,
Douglass used it as another tool in his crusade. He started
his own abolitionist newspaper, *The North Star,* with the
motto "Right is of no Sex–Truth is of no color–God is the
Father of us all, and we are all Brethren," and used it to
express his political and social theories. He was the first
black freeman in the United States to own a printing press.

As he continued to write and travel, Douglass real-
ized that the public needed something more personal

which would expose the ugliness of slavery, going beyond secondhand accounts and rumors of plantation life. This realization prompted Douglass to write his autobiography.

In 1845, when Douglass was twenty-seven, his book was published. The genre of the slave narrative was not unknown; there were over one hundred narratives in circulation before the end of the Civil War. However, most of these narratives were transcribed by abolitionists from accounts told to them by individuals who had escaped from slavery. These narratives were attacked as untruthful or exaggerated. Douglass's *Narrative of the Life of Frederick Douglass, Written by Himself,* was not only direct and informative, but the facts could be verified: The names he used in the book belonged to real people, and the descriptions of the events were accurate. For this reason, *Narrative* was a dangerous book. It was also a very successful book.

Douglass's writing style produced not only a well-constructed work of literature but also an emotionally forceful story. As William Lloyd Garrison stated, "He who can peruse it [*Narrative*] without a tearful eye, a heaving breast, an afflicted spirit,—without trembling for the fate of this country . . . must have a flinty heart." Simple and descriptive, without embellishment, *Narrative* achieves its purpose of informing the reader.

Douglass continued to speak and write, and ten years after the publication of his first book, his second autobiography, *My Bondage and My Freedom,* added details, particularly those of his escape to freedom, to the first account. This, too, sold well. However, his third autobiography, *Life and Times of Frederick Douglass,* was not as successful.

Douglass never gave up on his battle against slavery. An idealist until the end, Douglass transcended his era. His *Narrative* and his life's work are not only about the personal experience of slavery; they are about the importance of freedom. Douglass's belief that freedom is not a luxury but a human right still moves his readers as much today as it did over a hundred years ago.

■ ■ ■